Advance Praise for Intelligent Life in the Classroom

Rarely do I find an academic book that is a page-turner, but this one surely is! Karen and Tamara have addressed the identifying characteristics of gifted children through anecdotes that make the children come alive. At the same time, they provide excellent information for teachers on how to recognize salient characteristics and address gifted children's needs. This book is immensely readable but addresses the issues in an intellectually honest way. I know that my graduate students will love it, too.
—Bonnie Cramond, Ph.D., Professor,
   Department of Educational Psychology and Instructional
   Technology, and Director, Torrance Center for Creativity and
   Talent Development, University of Georgia

Intelligent Life in the Classroom gives teachers permission to appreciate and run with their gifted students' idiosyncrasies, interests, and divergent thinking. This practical book introduces teachers to the wonderful world of teaching gifted children.
—Dina Brulles, Ph.D. President,
   Arizona Association for Gifted and Talented, and Director of
   Gifted Education, Paradise Valley Unified School District, Arizona

Isaacson and Fisher have contributed a refreshingly welcome perspective concerning the complexities of smart kids and the teachers who reach them. Their lively writing style, attention to important issues, and use of substantive examples offer the reader a wealth of practical knowledge and strategies for working with gifted youth. Quite simply, an enjoyable, enlightening, must read for educators and parents.
—Marcia Gentry, Ph.D., Associate Professor, College of Education,
   and Associate Director, Gifted Education Resource Institute,
   Purdue University

D1115797

Intelligent Life in the Classroom:

Smart Kids and Their Teachers

by
Karen L. J. Isaacson
and
Tamara J. Fisher

Great Potential Press, Inc.
Scottsdale, Arizona

Copy editing: Jen Ault
Cover design: MWVelgos Design
Interior design: The Printed Page

Published by Great Potential Press, Inc.
P.O. Box 5057
Scottsdale, AZ 85261

Printed on recycled paper

© 2007 by Great Potential Press

11 10 09 08 07   5 4 3 2 1

Library of Congress Cataloging-in-Publication Data

Isaacson, Karen L.J., 1965-
    Intelligent life in the classroom : smart kids and their teachers / by
Karen L. J. Isaacson and Tamara J. Fisher.
        p. cm.
    Includes bibliographical references.
    ISBN 0-910707-75-8 (pbk.)
    1. Gifted children—Education—United States. 2. Creative ability in
children—United States. 3. Creative ability—Study and teaching
—United States.   I. Fisher, Tamara J., 1973-   . II. Title.
LC3993.9.I83 2007
371.95—dc22

                                        2006026728

ISBN 13: 978-0-910707-75-6
ISBN 10: 0-910707-75-8

Karen's Acknowledgements

First and always, my thanks go to my husband and my children for their support, their patience, and their very being. Without you guys, nothing else would matter. Next in line, I owe a great debt of gratitude to my grandmother and to my mother for their wisdom, experience, and willingness to share both. I've learned so much! To my coauthor, Tamara, thank you for being so wonderful to work with and having just the right personality to mesh with mine as we worked together on this project. My publishers Jan and Jim, thanks for your patience and your advice. I also owe a thank-you to several teachers and friends who made contributions to this book, among whom, to mention a few, are Laurie Martinez, Neena Packer, Kelle Bradshaw, Maureen Durso, Kathy Dufresne, Kathie Bailey, Autumn O'Brien, Callie Embry, and Kathy Cassidy.

Tamara's Acknowledgements

I wish to extend a heartfelt thanks to my students, who intrigue, inspire, and amaze me daily. Your ideas and stories give a needed voice to the thoughts, feelings, and experiences of gifted kids everywhere. I am also grateful to the Polson School District for allowing me creative freedom and flexibility in the development of a gifted program. I thank the parents and teachers of my students for sharing their perceptive stories about gifted youngsters. Thank you to my classmates from my Master's program for your enduring encouragement and support. To Karen, my coauthor, I extend a big thank-you for being a mentor and a friend. Jan and Jim of Great Potential Press, thank you for your insights. And I of course must thank my family for their love and for challenging me and nurturing my creative spirit. You are my heroes.

Contents

 Foreword

These days, pressures compel teachers to cover a prescribed list of content in a set time span with students whom we seldom really "see" because their presence has become secondary to the imperative of test preparation. Great teachers resist that process because it has as little to do with teaching as it does with learning.

Great teachers celebrate *who* they teach. They know that the light switches of learning must be flipped on in one brain at a time. They sense the magic that happens for any student who suddenly—or imperceptibly—realizes the power of mind to make meaning and the power of meaning to enrich life.

Great teachers also celebrate *what* they teach. They themselves are inspired by the relevance, interconnectedness, mystery, and evolution of ideas. Such teachers find personal meaning in what they learn. Through what they learn, they develop a spiraling appreciation of the world, and they are compelled to share the journey with young people who are just beginning it.

Teaching happens only when we realize it is the teacher's role to connect particular kids with dynamic content. Great teaching happens when we understand what makes a subject vibrate with possibilities, when we understand that no two students are identical as learners, and when we act on student differences to make sure each student has the greatest opportunity to learn the maximum amount possible about the electricity and connectivity of the disciplines.

In this book, written for teachers, a teacher and a parent are co-celebrants of the kids we teach. A joint teacher-parent authorship—though entirely right—is something of a rarity. Teachers (after a time) develop a breadth of understanding of students at a given developmental point that parents can seldom garner. At the same time, parents have a depth of knowledge of particular students that teachers can only dream of acquiring. Together, a parent and a teacher can paint, both with a broad brush *and* with fine lines.

These two authors do exactly that in ways that are meaningful, poignant, and often humorous.

Karen Isaacson and Tamara Fisher are connoisseurs of young learners, studying and savoring the variety of kids who come their way. They remind readers of a number of non-negotiables of superior teaching. Among the key concepts that stayed with me long after I closed the book are these:

- Learning happens when learners are inspired, not when they are admonished.

- Curiosity is a powerful motivator for learning.

- Kids come in different wrappers, with different ingredients and different eyes.

- Wise teachers study what sparks their students, both individually and collectively.

- Excellent teachers both follow and lead their students.

- The teachers we remember help us build lives, not data sheets.

- Great teaching shoots high and provides the support necessary for kids to exceed their dreams.

- Memorable teachers help students answer "So what?" about what they learn.

▦ Good teachers help students develop disciplined minds without overcoming students with discipline.

For me, this book is about teachers who go to school every day with an agenda for learning and a clear intent to be flexible within the perimeter of the agenda. It's about teachers who never, even in a long career, find two days alike. They know that, even if they taught the same thing for three decades, the students who need to learn it will be kaleidoscopic in their interactions with the content.

Intelligent Life in the Classroom reminds me of teachers who dealt with me and my classmates as though we were intelligent (even when that was a stretch)—and in doing so called out of us more than we thought was there. This book renews my intent as a teacher to be a catalyst for finding, affirming, and extending intelligence in my own students. I am pleased that these authors are sharing their wisdom, and humor, with other teachers.

Carol Ann Tomlinson, Ed.D.
Professor of Educational Leadership,
Foundations, and Policy
Curry School of Education
The University of Virginia

Karen's Preface

I have memories of sitting in a classroom in front of teachers whom I considered all-knowing and all-wonderful. Of course, there were always a few teachers who didn't fit that mold and gave me different memories. For example, in my eighth-grade Algebra class, I remember challenging myself by holding my breath and watching the clock to see if I could break my record. It was a terrific way to make time pass. However, it's always possible that this may have had more to do with the subject than the teacher.

At any rate, I remember most of my teachers with positive thoughts. I can still picture them as clear as day—okay, maybe their images are a little fuzzy around the edges, but you get the idea. They had a huge impact on me. Each personality was different, and each one affected me in a different way. Some made me feel loved, which I desperately needed, as I felt like such an oddity at times. Some made me work harder, which I also desperately needed. Some made every effort to showcase my talents—they made *me* feel needed. Then there were some teachers I may not have liked, but they opened up a whole new world of literature for me or introduced me to fascinating stories from history.

Now, as a mother of five, I appreciate the roles of teachers in a totally new way. Every weekday, I send my children off to school and entrust them to adults I know little about. Even with parent/teacher conferences, volunteering at the school, attending open houses, and listening to chatter between parents, as well as the feedback of my own children, I will never get to know these teachers well.

In working with Tamara to coauthor this book, I have had the opportunity to talk to teachers in much greater depth than I have ever had before, and I am grateful for it. And I have had the opportunity to tell teachers some of what I desperately want them to know.

I have teachers in my family. My grandmother taught for several years in California, and she provided me with some great stories for this book; she also provided me with a lifetime of experience from a truly gifted teacher. My mother spent several years working with bright and talented children, developing programs and curriculum to meet their needs. I've included some of her stories as well.

I also interviewed teachers to add their experiences to this book. As I listened to each story, each laugh, each sigh, each positive comment, I was impressed and awed by teachers' abilities and their challenges.

Now that I'm an adult, I still have a difficult time calling teachers by their first names. Unless I know them well, I always use their full titles—Mr. Gutierrez, Mrs. Jackson, Ms. Llewellyn. It all goes back to those days when I sat in front of those omniscient authorities on every subject, at least as far as my little brain was concerned. That influence and respect lasts a lifetime.

Tamara's Preface

After turning in a math test when I was in first grade, and having double-checked my answers as I had been well-trained to do, I sat back down at my desk to wait quietly for the other kids to finish. As boredom set in, my eyes caught a glimpse of the shiny new scissors nestled in the pencil tray inside my desk. I slyly slipped them out of the desk and began playing with them, admiring the light reflecting off the blades and how they worked. Of course I had to test them out. Well, next day was picture day. Despite my mother's attempts to conceal my lack of hairstyling skills, crooked bangs and a braid that went missing are still quite apparent in my picture from that year.

Now that I'm a teacher, this is the sort of story I relay to my students periodically because it helps them know that I'm human; I've been where they are. I love being a teacher, and although I considered many other career options, I think I always came back to teaching because it was the one option where I could be a little bit of everything: social worker, interior decorator, police officer, nurse, counselor, researcher, cartoonist, historian, editor, attorney, statistician, and writer.

I was also inspired by many of my own teachers over the years. A few of them motivated my career choice because I sat in their classes thinking of better or more creative or challenging ways to teach the lesson. But most of them inspired me with their incredible talents and wisdom and by the many positive and profound ways in which they touched and shaped my life. I try to live up to their examples each day, and it is an honor not only to follow in their footsteps, but also to branch off in my own direction.

I teach in a small town on an Indian Reservation in Montana, and my job is to be teacher and coordinator, K-12, for the gifted and talented program in our district. Native American children are often underrepresented in gifted programs around the country, and many Reservation schools don't even have GT programs; I'm honored to be a part of a system that supports such a program. Many non-Indian people live here, too, so our schools are an integrated mix of both Indian and non-Indian.

Since I am the only Gifted Education Specialist for our four schools, I work with these students for multiple consecutive years. This means that I am able to establish long-term connections with them and that I get to know their learning needs really well. Over the years, this consistency has helped me develop a better understanding of the "evolution of a gifted child" from kindergarten through high school. By sharing stories of my experiences with these students, I hope to relate the most important things I've learned—with hopes that you will gain a deeper understanding of the gifted students in your classrooms.

As a teacher, you know that, despite our college and university education and training, teaching involves a good dose of on-the-job training. When it comes to teaching gifted students, this seems to be even truer. How much did any of us learn about gifted students in our teacher preparation programs? If your experience was like mine and those of most teachers I know, the answer is practically nothing. Although I believe that my undergraduate degree program prepared me well for teaching in general, it is not where I learned about teaching gifted students. I clearly remember the *one* day in our "Exceptional Needs" course in which we spent 15 minutes (yes, *15 minutes*) on the topic of gifted and talented children. Not that the other varieties of exceptional needs that we learned about (in *far* greater depth) weren't important; they were. But it's no wonder we all ended up rather baffled about these oddball, quirky, gifted kids who outpace not only their classmates, but also their teachers. No one gave us a head's up that these kids would be in our classrooms, and no one gave us any clue about how to work with them, either.

Thankfully, there are now more ways teachers can learn more about teaching gifted students. Courses in how to create rigorous curriculum are becoming more common, and more and more states and universities are offering special endorsements in Gifted Education, which usually means about 18 hours of coursework, sometimes more. We stand on the shoulders of giants because a lot of progress has been made in this field. But there's still a long way to go.

Writing this book with Karen has been a great opportunity for me to assist teachers everywhere in beginning their own journey of learning about gifted students. Whether you are new to this journey or are many miles ahead of me, I'm happy to be on the road with you.

Teaching gifted children and advocating for their needs has proven to be far more challenging, varied, and fulfilling than I had ever hoped it would be. These children are *more* of everything—more curious, more energetic, more challenging, more sensitive, more intense, more perceptive, and more divergent. Consequently, they have high expectations of me as their teacher. I am always assured of a very rigorous day as I try to keep up with them!

1: All That Potential

"That students differ may be inconvenient, but it is inescapable."
~ Theodore Sizer ~

As a teacher, are you curious about a slightly odd, quirky child in your classroom? Concerned for the brainy loner who doesn't fit in? Or the slightly irritating student who asks an avalanche of questions? Are you struggling to challenge the student who seems to already know everything you were planning to teach?

You've no doubt discovered that teaching the gifted child in your classroom is not the cakewalk you thought it might be. Chances are that this student challenges you at every turn, or displays behaviors that leave you shaking your head in bewilderment, or is so focused on keeping the peace on the playground that she is seen as bossy by the other kids. You find yourself explaining to the parents that their student would have easy straight A's if only the homework made it from his desk to yours. Ah, yes! You're beginning to realize that a gifted child's potential also comes with quite a potential for worry and headaches.

Never fear. You're a teacher! You believe in the power of education. And just as you aim for learning and fun to go hand-in-hand in your classroom, we aim for the same in this book.

Whether you teach in a regular classroom and deal with identified (or not yet identified) gifted children as a part of a

1

larger group, or whether you work with gifted children in pull-out groups or special classrooms, we hope this book will help you gain a better understanding of gifted children in all their forms and varieties. We also hope this book will help you better unlock and stimulate the potential of those gifted minds, as well as deal with all of the other issues that are so often a part of these children who are unique in certain ways.

If you are reading this book, then it's obvious that you have an interest in learning more about giftedness and how it affects the students you work with. You probably want to learn what they look and act like and how to interact with them. You may wonder if you'll be able to answer their questions. Or whether they'll know more about some things than you, their teacher. Your interest and curiosity and desire to learn is an important first step on the road to being not merely a teacher who can work with gifted students, but a "gifted teacher," meaning you will use your creative abilities to provide an exciting learning environment, that you will use your understanding of giftedness to reach and communicate with your students on their level, and that you will understand and accept them for who they are. We believe these same skills will help improve classrooms for *all* students, whatever their learning level.

We are well aware that the phrase "gifted teacher" is commonly used in many schools to refer to the teacher of the gifted, or the gifted specialist. But we want to be clear here that our use of the phrase extends to *all* kinds of teachers—whatever their current teaching assignment. When we talk of "gifted teachers," we are referring to all teachers who are gifted in what they do, no matter what kind of students they teach.

Our chapter headings feature some of the most commonly acknowledged traits and characteristics of gifted children. We will look at each one with an eye toward understanding how a trait manifests in a gifted child and another eye toward finding some humor in the situation.

How will you know if you have a gifted child in your classroom? Using a David Letterman-type strategy, let's count down on a few predictions. Since we live and work in Montana, keep in mind that some of the statements could have a Montana flavor.

You probably have a gifted child in your classroom if:

10. He brings to class the heart from the deer his dad shot while hunting over the weekend...to Show and Tell, and he brings it pre-sliced to highlight each ventricle and valve.

9. She decides to stay in during recess to organize the art supplies in your classroom by color, type, texture, size, and availability.

8. He can explain in detail everything there is to know about different types of stars, but he can't find the pencil on the floor beneath his feet—even when you point directly to it.

7. She befriends the loneliest student because she doesn't want to turn him away like all of the other kids do.

6. His brain and his body are moving 100 miles an hour morning to night, 24 hours a day, seven days a week, and he hasn't figured out how to slow down when it's necessary to do so.

5. She aces tests but won't raise her hand in class because she doesn't want the other kids to know how smart she actually is.

4. He volunteers at the local nursing home where he reads to elderly patients, but he won't sign up for credit for his volunteer hours because he doesn't want the other kids to know what he's doing and think he's "soft" or "a sissy."

3. Her vocabulary is far more extensive than yours.

2. His imagination runs wild, especially when he creates constructions with his K'NEX® sets. He's been sleeping on the couch lately because his bedroom is literally filled floor to ceiling with his designs.

1. She has a secret notebook filled with poetry and short stories that she has illustrated, and she only showed it to you because you mentioned you like to draw.

Gifted students are different from the average student and stand out as "exceptional" in some way. It might be in academics; it might be in empathy or concern for a cause; it might be a special area of interest or ability or talent. They aren't "better" than other children, because every child is special and deserves to reach his highest potential, but gifted children *do* learn differently—a lot faster, for one thing—and like to learn more about things. If they get interested in something, they may want to learn all they can about that topic. So teachers just need to help them find more information. It doesn't mean you have to learn everything there is to know about dolphins yourself; just help Hector access more information, and then let him loose with it.

As gifted teachers—whether we are teaching in a classroom full of gifted students or a class of mixed-ability students—we cannot take the conventional route, because we are not dealing with conventional factors. We are in an exceptional and critical situation in which we are influencing and nurturing minds, souls, futures, dreams, and unknowable potentials.

It's all in that neat little package sitting at the desk in front of you, swinging legs, chewing on hair, or reading a novel during your carefully prepared geography lesson.

In our book, we use some famous gifted people to help us illustrate our points—as well as to help you see the potential in each of your students. For example, we mention Pearl Buck, Thomas Edison, and Leonardo da Vinci. You never know what direction a student will pursue or what she will do with her life as an adult, but the worth and potential of each little soul is immeasurable.

While we're talking about students, we want to mention here that student names in this book have been changed to protect the innocent, as well as the not-so-innocent. You can be assured the stories are real, however, even though the names are not.

We know that some students are easier to work with than others. You will love some students; others will challenge you to your breaking point; and still others will break your heart because there is no reason to believe that anyone but you cares about them at all.

We want to encourage you. We want to empathize with you. We want to give *you* every advantage when it comes to understanding gifted children, their quirks, their potentials, and their foibles.

Great teaching lessons do not come in kits or teacher books. Great teachers do not come in the same packages. Colleges and universities can't stamp them out on the assembly lines and produce uniform quality products. Great teachers arise when the average teacher chooses to put her whole heart and soul into the education of maturing minds, and when she looks beyond the surface of each face and into the brain gears and wheels that whir and tick, and when she expands her own knowledge of the special needs of children with differing strengths, abilities, weaknesses, and challenges.

Great teachers have the ability to develop strong relationships with their students as individuals and as a group. They love them. They accept and understand them. They speak their language. They know how to reach out with their brains and touch the brains of the learner. And they're humble enough to know that they are (still and always) a learner, too.

Gifted teachers love what they teach. They love what they learn. They love all of the questions about all of the stuff they know and all of the stuff they are clueless about. They're curious. They're creative. They're not afraid of unexpected situations, because they recognize those situations as opportunities. "What can I learn from this?" "How can I solve that?" "How can I motivate this bright kid?"

Teachers would certainly like to receive a larger salary, and they deserve to earn far more than they do. But even if they weren't paid to teach, most teachers would still want to teach; they just can't help it. Wherever they are or whatever else they may do, it will probably involve some form of teaching. A gifted teacher sorting peas on an assembly line would probably say to the person next to him, "Did you know peanuts are also called *goober peas?* Do you know all the uses George Washington Carver discovered for peanuts?"

Teachers are not clones. They are not stereotypes. They are as unique and wonderful as the little people they work with. Teachers are just people who have a green thumb for helping brains to grow to their maximum potential!

2: Curiosity

If we took a poll to discover history's most curious man—the inquisitive kind of "curious," not curious as in "odd"—one of the top contenders would be Leonardo da Vinci. Nothing was beyond his ponderings and exploration, from architecture to zoology, anatomy to mathematics, astronomy to weaponry, engineering to painting. His inquiry was often centuries ahead of his time, with inventions that sometimes required the world to catch up with him first in order for them to come to fruition. He devoured books and took advantage of any opportunity that appealed to his curiosity. Leonardo even skirted the laws of humanity and society by dissecting cadavers in order to learn anatomy, long before a legal process was developed for such scientific study. He annoyed his teachers with his endless questions and was so curious that he went against his own values in some instances so that he could follow a question until he was satisfied. For Leonardo, the need to satisfy curiosity was paramount.

Let's send the young Master da Vinci on a little time traveling experiment. Let's bring him forward into our current educational system, and then let's send him backward to the age of nine. We imagine he might be a little dizzy after all of this back and forth business, but we think he's up for it. Let's imagine you teach third grade, and lucky you, little Leo is in your class. He sits in the front seat in the center of the classroom. He is never quiet, because when he isn't asking questions, you can hear the gnawing sounds of teeth on a No. 2 pencil as his brain grinds away on something else. You are unable to finish any lesson as planned because young Leo interrupts with questions—some appropriate, and some so bizarre that you can't make the connection to the current subject. Frustrating? Yes. Is it tempting to tell the kid to sit tight and nix the questions so the other kids can learn? Well, yes, it is.

So if Leo is sitting in your classroom today, that means his brilliant—if somewhat annoying—high-powered brain has access to today's technology. We know what he did with the technology available to him in the 1400s; we can only imagine what someone like Leonardo would do with the information available today. Where would his brain take him? Where would it take us?

Now imagine this. What if this incredibly inquisitive, brilliant mind were required to stay with his age peers and learn from a standard, structured curriculum that didn't fit his needs? Let's imagine he already understands all of the math taught in third grade and is certainly far beyond other classmates in his ability to conceptualize things in sketches and drawings. And what if he received no opportunities to work with mentors who were recognized experts in their fields, as he did more than 500 years ago?

Something went right for Leonardo's curiosity back in 1462. Are there some ways we can make it go right for the curiosity of all bright children today? So many questions. But then, this is a chapter on curiosity.

Karen remembers being full of questions as a young girl. She usually had more questions than the teacher had time to answer. Back when she was in first grade, the second most magical thing for her (after learning to read) was seeing, or rather hearing, a tape recorder for the first time. She had never seen or heard of such a machine before. Today, she often sits at a computer but says it doesn't feel nearly as magical as that first brush, years ago, with technology—the tape recorder. Mrs. Stodgebottom, her first-grade teacher, allowed each of her students to record their names and a brief message, and then she played it back to them. Karen was thrilled for the whole nine seconds that she heard herself speak. The only problem was that the teacher played it back for the class only once. That was it. Well, Karen was dying to hear her own voice again. It was difficult to believe that it even belonged to her, that voice. And she was enthralled with the magical little box with buttons and knobs that had made it all possible. So while the voice of her teacher hummed on in the front of the classroom about their next math assignment, Karen, who couldn't have cared less right then about one plus one and two plus two, was wondering, "What other things could I do with that tape recorder?" All her little brain could think about was the magical object. How did it work? Was that really her voice? *Really?* Could it record her voice from far away? How far? What would she sound like when she sang? Or when she made scary monster sounds? Could she use it to spy on people? What if it could record other things besides sound? Could she change her voice on it? What was inside of the black plastic box? What was inside the tape? Did it have writing on it that the machine could read?

She didn't dare mention any of this to her teacher, Mrs. Stodgebottom. She wouldn't have understood. But gifted teachers understand. They remember the magic of children's curiosity.

Karen always dreamed of a classroom full of junk that no one wants any more—computers, cameras, TVs, tape recorders, telephones, telescopes, and gadgets of every description. Or other stuff. Books on lots of subjects. Hands-on nature things like birds' nests or all sorts of rocks. To her, that would be Kid Paradise: a room full of things you can look at, touch, or take apart to see how they work, where no one is worried you're going to break something.

Can you imagine yourself as a kid walking into a classroom like that? Lots of cool stuff everywhere? Then add an adult who loves to answer kids' questions and lead the children to find their own answers. Then take it one step farther and add a reference library on a child's level explaining how things work so students can look things up if they have questions. Throw in a few simple tools to help them out. Imagine the experimenting and the hands-on experiences that could happen in a classroom like that! Kids would be playing with gears, turning them around in fascination just to watch the chain reaction and seeing what they could add to it or how they could use it for something else. Each child would be learning at his own pace, with information planted firmly and in context. That would be one cool classroom.

On the other hand, you *could* open up a science textbook to a chapter on levers, wheels, and inclined planes; give a brief lecture with some discussion; and assign some vocabulary words, due at the beginning of class Thursday morning, pencil only— no ink. You see our point.

Home school parents talk about "unschooling" as an approach to education. It means, simply, freeing the child from set times to do certain assigned subjects and allowing her to learn what she wants to learn based on her interests, with the parent (with the help of the public library and the wider community) providing the activities and materials. While this may not be practical for the classroom in which students are required to take standardized tests or learn a pre-set curriculum, the idea can be modified to fit the classroom requirements. For example, when young scientists are scheduled to learn about inclined planes and levers, the teacher can take some classroom time to explain the basic principles and also allow the children some free time to explore a collection of everyday objects—objects which include inclined planes or levers—on their own. They can play with them, hands-on, and see where and how those simple machines add up to more complicated processes. Give them enough information and structure to ensure that they will grasp the required information, and then mix it with a little curiosity about how things work to help them find a permanent place for that information in their brains. When knowledge is *their* discovery, they will feel as though they own it.

We probably don't give children enough credit for being able to answer their own questions. We may even be afraid, at times, of where their curiosity will lead them. While they do require some guidance, it is amazing to see what they can do and where they will go when they are given the freedom to explore those subjects they are curious about.

When Mrs. Carmichael began her first year of teaching gifted students in the pull-out program, she (naturally) didn't know (yet) what she was doing. She had a group of gifted seventh and eighth graders to work with, and she wasn't sure quite how she was going to challenge them. So she brainstormed with the class, and together they decided they were going to build a model-sized solar car and a windmill. Wow! This was a tall order. It was sure to be a challenge, since Mrs. Carmichael had no idea how they would go about this project.

The next time they met, Mrs. Carmichael, due to confusion on her part—which is normal for gifted teachers—came to class 25 minutes late. The kids were already up at the whiteboard and had decided that they weren't going to build a solar car or windmill after all, but instead, they were going to put Goldilocks (from the children's story with the three bears) on trial for trespassing, breaking and entering, destruction of property, theft, and yes, even murder. Apparently, they imagined, Goldilocks had blood on her hands and was on the lam when she discovered the bears' house. Mrs. Carmichael was hesitant at first but decided to let them follow their own ideas. The goal, after all, was to let the students have some say in what they wanted to study and learn, and she was all for that. The kids ran with it. One of the "lawyers" decided to investigate the different types of wood used in the broken chairs as he built a defense for

Goldilocks. Cheap wood would break into a jillion pieces easily enough.

It was during this time that DNA testing was first used in Montana to convict a man for murder. There was no body, but a tiny bit of tissue was found on the side of a camper, and DNA testing was used to identify it as belonging to the suspected victim. So Mrs. Carmichael decided to bring the new detective tool into the classroom somehow and told her students that the case would have to be based on the use of DNA testing. There was no murder in the original Goldilocks story, but they decided to add one to make things more interesting. Mrs. Carmichael gave them some guidelines to make sure the case didn't get gruesome and turn into a Saturday Night Movie.

The students now had a theoretical body to dispose of, and they debated the possibilities for some time. About two weeks later, two of the boys came tearing into class, saying, "Mrs. Carmichael, did you know that a pot-bellied pig can eat a human body, bones and everything?" She was, of course, duly amazed. So pot-bellied pigs entered the story as a creative method of destroying evidence. The class made a conference call to one of the local laboratories and asked how many pot-bellied pigs it would take to consume a 150-pound body. They determined it would take four pigs.

Subsequently, the lawyers in the mock trial queried the potential jurors in their most serious voices with questions like, "Do you or any members of your family eat bacon?" and "How do you feel about pigs?"

The case took over a semester to finish and turned out to be far more interesting and involved than any of the students or the teacher had ever thought possible. While it was going on, this teacher of gifted students was afraid she would get phone calls from concerned parents asking what in the world she was teaching their children. Instead, what she got, after the whole thing was over, was parents who were amazed at how excited the kids were about the case and how they would jump in the car and go to do their assignments.

Whereas all kids are curious, gifted kids show intense curiosity and can totally immerse themselves in something that interests them. In fact, they may not want to move on to other subjects if they are still fascinated by the thing that interests them at the moment.

What did these legal investigators learn? They learned interview skills, research skills, organizational skills, planning skills, critical thinking, and questioning skills. And perhaps, most important, they learned how to follow their curiosity and interests and learn something without a basal text telling them what facts to study. They learned how to learn on their own by thinking and using their brains.

Curiosity can light many unexpected and fascinating fires. It can also be used to make other less interesting subjects more exciting to individual students.

Let's think for a moment about that smart kid we all know who hates history but loves math. Let's make history real and important to him by bringing in all sorts of math, which, by the way, will also be useful in answering that timeless question— "When am I ever going to use this stuff?" Let's see. Do battle plans require math? How about the Romans' methods of determining voting districts? How much time did it take for Columbus to cross the ocean? How many miles did he average per day? How much food did they eat per person per day, and how much room did it take to store it? How much would that cost in today's market? Big numbers. But kids like to say, "Wow!" Listen to them. It's one of their favorite words. Bring the "wow" into your classroom as often as you can. Amazing things earn these kids' respect. That's why *Ripley's Believe It Or Not!*® is so successful.

There are no isolated subjects in real life. Why should the subjects taught in school be any different? Each story has the potential of introducing thousands of questions—questions just dying for answers—and those questions and answers will give birth to even more questions. What an incredible world we live in!

Skip the conventional and go for the interesting. Take the path less traveled rather than the path of least resistance. Pretend that no other teacher or textbook writer has gone before you to mark the way, and you are the first. You can have the same goal, but you don't necessarily have to have the same method. How would you go about getting the information across? Can you take your ideas and make them even better?

Yes, we realize that you have to stick with a prescribed curriculum and teach what's in the curriculum, but you can use the natural curiosity of the children to enhance their interest levels in the subject and to give the information context, which will actually give them a reason to remember what the textbook says. They need a reason. They need to *want* to know.

And even if you can't take much class time to pursue a subject further, there's no reason why you can't stimulate their interest and their brains in a way that will encourage them to pursue a subject in more depth on their own time. For the gifted kids who have already mastered parts of the curriculum, they can "buy time" to pursue these interests by compacting out of the lessons they don't need. (Resources with information on curriculum compacting are listed at the end of the book.)

In *Cheaper by the Dozen*,[1] Mr. Gilbreth, the father, takes every opportunity to teach his children. Mr. Gilbreth is an excellent example of someone who teaches by using the natural curiosity of the student. He writes messages in Morse Code on the walls. He has a daughter named Ernestine, and one of the phrases he writes in code is, "Two maggots were fighting in dead earnest." His wife may not have appreciated that morbid humor at her child's expense, but one child we know thought it was absolutely hilarious. It was certainly more clever and interesting than the message in the movie *The Christmas Story*, when poor Ralphie finally receives the secret decoder for the "Little

Orphan Annie" radio show, and the only message he can decode is, "Be sure to drink your Ovaltine®!"[2]

When Karen was younger—much, much, younger—she used to dream about being able to write codes and someday grow up to be a spy. Her curiosity was taking her in a direction. She practiced as much as possible, but it wasn't very satisfactory, since there was very little to spy on at her house. (Maybe it was the same in your house.) Nevertheless, she used to hide in closets to discover the secrets of her younger siblings, and not long after that, she and her brother Myron discovered that the wall between the closets was nothing more than a thin piece of plywood, and they could easily drill a little peephole through that. Keep in mind that they were fairly young, and their siblings were even younger, so there wasn't much to see that Karen and Myron hadn't already seen, as toddlers usually ran around the house half-naked anyway. Still, no one could convince Karen and Myron that maybe those little innocents weren't possible spies for dark forces that were hiding in the disguise of a three-year-old little sister. It was their duty to find out. Karen was busy experimenting with different interests.

She also admits that, during her spying days, she listened to downstairs conversations through the upstairs heater vents. She'd like to be able to say that she heard revealing tidbits, but she usually heard very little. But the point is that kids love, love, love mysteries—mysteries of all sorts, shapes, and subjects. It appeals to their curious side. You can serve mystery liberally in just about any subject, and they'll eat it up. If there's a good question and a good mystery to solve, you'll have their interest.

Ms. O'Neill, a teacher of the gifted—also a gifted teacher—walked into her classroom one day to find that a group of her students had arrived early and were huddled around something in the corner. She soon discovered that they were conducting an experiment to solve The Janitor Mystery. The "classroom" was actually a small room in an out-of-the-way location. Getting to the room required walking through the office. (Teachers who are specialists rather than regular classroom teachers often get the leftovers when it comes to space; they sometimes get a large storage closet.) Ms. O'Neill and her students noticed that the janitor wasn't coming around each night to clean their space. Janitors work really hard, so they were sure he was just missing them because of their out-of-the-way location. Well, the students found a way to know if he had finally cleaned their room. "What are you kids doing over there on the floor?" Caught red-handed, no one spoke up. Ms. O'Neill pried them away from the corner and discovered a hunk of cheese on the floor. What?! Yes, there was a hunk of dried up cheese on the floor between the desk and the bookshelf. After some mild interrogation, she discovered that some of her students had hidden it there weeks before to test whether the janitor cleaned their area. Curiosity is a big factor in detective work.

One of Tamara's students, Vijay, was curious about something. He didn't let cold, wet, or adverse conditions stop his curiosity, either. He and his family often took walks together along the lakeshore. One winter, after a bit of a thaw, there were small pools of water within the ice along the shore. Vijay noticed bubbles coming up in the middle of the pools, and he was curious about what was making them. He began digging until he found the source—a crayfish. He found the answer. It was true discovery learning.

We hear stories of gifted kids who drive their parents crazy taking things apart so they can see how they work. We've heard of young children digging up a lawn sprinkler system or taking apart a vacuum cleaner—both rather dirty and messy tasks—to see how they work. Taking apart a phone or a radio is one thing—as long as it's not plugged into a wall or is someone else's property. But please don't let children open the back of your computer! Some of these things can be seriously dangerous. A child needs a parent or teacher to help watch for safe opportunities for him to explore.

As a famous tabloid says, "Inquiring minds want to know!" Kids start inquiring as soon as they can form questions. Why is the sky blue? Why do we have fingernails? Why do I have to make my bed when I'm only going to mess it up again tonight? Their brains yearn to learn. They want, and expect, answers.

So curiosity is a fabulous learning tool that should be used liberally. Used properly, it's also a terrific tool for managing behavior.

Mrs. McGillicuddy had a group of young students who were advanced and needed something more in their curriculum, as they had the reading thing down pat. Some of them had become behavior problems in class, possibly because they were bored. Mrs. McGillicuddy decided that this would be a great time to start them on microscopes. She went around and borrowed every unused microscope she could find. She spent very little money.

The high school science teacher gave her a bunch of plastic slides that he had no use for. You would have thought it was a thousand-dollar science kit, the way those young kids were looking through the old broken-down microscopes at cotton cloth and single threads. Before they looked at the cotton or thread, they were asked to draw what they thought it would look like under the microscope. Their curiosity kicked in. What does cotton *really* look like when you get right down to the nitty-gritty itty bitty? They had no idea. Their original drawings each consisted of a single curved line, which is all they were able to see when they looked at that piece of thread at its actual size. They then looked through the microscope and drew what they saw. After they were finished, they were able to compare the two drawings. What a difference! Their curiosity was temporarily satisfied, even as new questions popped up. Did all cloth and all threads and fibers look the same as cotton? How were they different? They found similar samples and studied them—cloth and threads made from other fibers, both natural and synthetic, plus dog hair, cat hair, and their own hair. (They received instructions on the ethical methods for obtaining pet and human hair, thankfully.) It's amazing what 40 minutes with old microscopes twice a week can do. Not only did the kids enjoy the project, but also their behavior changed. Their brains were busy. Teachers commented on the improved behavior. Parents commented on how behavior at home had improved, too.

Give kids' brains something worthwhile to work on, and their attitudes can change. Don't give them the chance to ask themselves, "What can I do for excitement in the classroom? Pass me the spitwads!" Send their curiosity in another, more positive direction.

When we let children be curious, they ask questions like, "What if a hovercraft had wings?" "Do small changes in what I eat affect my performance on the football field?" "Why is Montana's western boundary so squiggly?" "How come identical twins don't have the same fingerprints?" "How does an illness affect a calf's growth and lifespan?" "Why are kids so mean to each other?" "What are the manmade causes of global warming, and what are the natural causes of it? Was there ever such a thing as global cooling, and was it considered to be a problem, too?"

Which is better? A disciplined, quiet classroom, or a noisy, free-form one? Well, there's no easy answer, other than there's probably a time and a place for various kinds of noise levels. When kids are excited, their voices generally go up in volume. If they're excited about what they're learning and doing and they're working well in their groups, that's all good. There's no rule that says a classroom should always be quiet.

A higher activity level, and sometimes more noise, are part of the package in Tamara's classroom of gifted students; it comes with the questions and fascinating conversations. Even while working on their independent projects, a steady stream of curious banter persists. Her students will eagerly pick up any topic of interest to them. They'll debate it and examine its multi-faceted viewpoints. When the bell rings and they head down the hallway, Tamara can hear them talking about the possibilities of their topic. Days or weeks later when the same topic is brought up once again, they pick up right where they left off, pressing each other for facts or new ideas, experimenting with their own questions by seeing how the others respond to them.

While it could be easy for a teacher to become annoyed by their endless curiosity—it can certainly distract from what is "supposed" to be happening in the classroom—Tamara has found herself impressed by the level of sophistication and the esteem in which these children hold a good question.

We heard somewhere that the average four-year-old asks 435 questions a day. Any mother of a four-year-old could probably verify that. It could also be argued that one reason four-year-olds learn so much is because they ask so many questions. So why doesn't the average 12-year-old ask 435 questions a day? What have we done? Have we squeezed curiosity out of our children? Discouraged their questions? Is it really so important that we say, "Don't interrupt me right now," so as to not be annoyed by children's persistent questions? Shouldn't it be more important that we nurture in them a healthy and natural curiosity that will lead them to asking the biggest and hardest questions of science, mathematics, literature, history, politics, and humanity? If we slap their wrists for being inconveniently curious, will they still be curious?

Leon Lederman,[3] a nuclear physicist, said, "Those who do not stop asking silly questions become scientists." We're pretty sure they also grow up to be historians and journalists and inventors and leaders.

Tamara's Advanced Studies class for gifted seventh through twelfth graders is an opportunity for curious students with burning questions to pursue them through independent study projects. Unfortunately, it seems there have become fewer and fewer opportunities for such pursuits in our classrooms over the last century. While she thinks that the reasons for this decline in curiosity may be due to: (1) an assembly line model of education, (2) bureaucratic restrictions, (3) a teacher's need for control of the classroom or image preservation, and/or (4) a culture which seems to tear down the "nerd," she makes every effort to keep curiosity alive in her classroom. Doing so means there will be messy days, raucous debates, mistakes, failures, steps backward, and uncomfortable moments. But it also means that her classroom is home to wonder, amazing successes, topic immersion, leaps forward, discovery, aspiration, and most importantly, ever-present curiosity.

Do we underestimate the children of the world? When Tamara began her position as Gifted Specialist for her school district, she knew she had very capable kids to work with. But until she let them roam free with their curiosity, until she opened to them the possibility of pursuing their own questions to the fullest extent, she had no idea just how much they were truly capable of. When she gives them some free reign with curiosity, she is consistently blown away by their ideas, questions, talents, and possibilities.

The wide variety of the independent projects they choose to investigate in the Advanced Studies class mirrors the curiosity these young people have for the world around them. Over the years, Tamara's students have taken on many topics in the form of a project, research study, or solution to a real-world problem. In order to satiate their curiosity, create a product, or research a question of importance to them, they have chosen to do— among many, *many* things—the following:

- take apart and rebuild a motor.
- compose their own songs, then burn them onto CDs for friends.
- write novels and send them to publishers.
- design and build an electric guitar…*from scratch*.
- create magazines and distribute them to hundreds of readers.
- build models of the chemical structures of various fungi.
- learn new languages such as Japanese and Latin.

- learn about some of their Native American culture, like beading, storytelling, or learning their native language.
- learn to play new instruments.
- research family or Tribal genealogy.
- breed and raise sheep.
- design and build new styles of bicycles and go-karts.
- build computers from scrapped parts.
- teach younger students in the district about magnetism, nutrition, writing, and countless other topics.
- film and edit their own movies.
- research diseases that affect calves after birth and write an informational booklet for area ranchers.
- create websites for local businesses.
- design and weld a kayak trailer for a bicycle.
- research how different cultures view and deal with death.
- design snowboards and have them actually made.

Each semester, Tamara wonders how the new group of students can possibly come up with new and unusual ideas, and yet each semester they do. Their minds are a whirlwind of new possibilities. And you can be sure that when they are adults, they will still remember that independent study project they did in that gifted class with that really cool teacher. The experience will etch itself in their memories. It was the process that was thrilling, that feeling of freedom to investigate and explore and use one's mind to come up with answers. As a matter of fact, one of the unexpected results is the high number of Tamara's students who go on to pursue a college major or career related to the topic of the independent project they did in Advanced Studies class.

Can you imagine how exciting it is to be a teacher whose curriculum is always new and exciting, even while it provides consistency and structure? Is it scary cutting them loose to pursue their own topics? Of course! Although for Tamara, after 10 years, it's not nearly as scary now as it was when she started.

Does it feel chaotic having so many students working on so many different topics at the same time in the same space? Oh yes, at times, but she also finds that they actually tend to be more focused in her classroom than in other settings.

Tamara has a two-drawer file cabinet in her classroom where she stores tools that the students can use for working on their projects. Because it includes utility knives and a handsaw, she keeps it locked to prevent outsiders from getting their paws on these little treasures. Her students know where the key is hidden so they can access the tools when they need them for their projects. At the beginning of class one day, Tamara noticed two of the boys in her class trying to pick the lock. "Ford and Cree, why are you doing that? Is the key missing?" "Oh, no, it's there, Miss Fisher, but getting in this way is more fun!" they said with the enthusiasm that comes only from exploring one's curiosity.

Tamara thought back to her college days when she had read a book written by Nobel Prize-winning physicist Richard P. Feynman. One of the stories in his book told of a time when he had attempted to crack some safes—not to be a thief, but rather because he was curious about their locking mechanisms and how their individual codes could be broken. It was Feynman's curiosity, evidenced in this and so many other areas, which eventually led him to make the discovery for which he later won the Nobel Prize. And here Tamara had two little Feynmans right in her own classroom. "Carry on, boys, carry on." Soon, the file cabinet was cracked open, and they transitioned to working on their projects with the needed tools.

It would've been easy to chastise them for their actions and stop their curious behavior. After all, do we want them picking other locks? Certainly not. But they weren't trying to pick locks in places they knew they weren't supposed to get into. They were only pursuing a new route to a place they already had permission to go. Maybe someday their curiosity will lead to an important discovery. Maybe, if their minds continue to be free to learn and discover to their heart's content, historians 500 years from now will write about them and their amazing contributions to humankind.

You will probably never know if you have a modern-day Feynman or Leonardo Da Vinci in your classroom, though you may have some good candidates. Only time will tell what your students will actually accomplish. But teachers hold an important key to freeing their students' curiosity, and therefore their potential. Some days you may have to toss the key aside and pick the lock—because it makes things more interesting. And maybe because *you* are a little curious as well.

3: Intensity

"One can never consent to creep when one feels an impulse to soar!"
~ Helen Keller ~

Nearly every observation-based method used to identify advanced learners or those we call "gifted" includes the word "intensity" or some version thereof as a key characteristic of gifted individuals. Parents of gifted children can verify this with countless stories. For example, when a gifted three-year-old boy pretends to be a squirrel, he isn't content to hop around the yard for the afternoon, pretending to waggle his tail and look for nuts. No, he has to sleep perched on his headboard at night, because that's the closest thing he can find to a tree limb, and he persists even after he falls off a time or two and wakes his parents.

As for gifted adults, we know of writers and scientists who spend 72 hours at a stretch working on a task at their desk or microscope, forgoing sleep until they reach a satisfactory conclusion or other stopping point. You may know some individuals like this or people with varying degrees of intensity. Some gifted experts believe that the level of intensity increases with the level of giftedness, or that the more highly gifted person will be the more intense individual.

Decades of research and anecdotal observation illustrate that many gifted individuals have a knack for "excesses,"—for being intense to an extreme about almost anything and everything.

These individuals are often considered by others to be "over the top" in their interests, expressions, commitments, avoidances, and energy levels. These are the people who can't let something go, can work on a project for 10 straight hours without a break, or can win any argument simply by wearing down the other person or debating them into exhaustion.

The Wright brothers pursued their goal of manned flight with such intensity that they slacked off in other important areas of their lives, like working at paying jobs and spending time with their families. They were practically laughed out of town as "crazies" because people thought their goal was simply impossible. People didn't understand the intensity with which they worked to succeed.

Gandhi pursued his political views with such intensity that he was willing to fast, nearly starving himself, to make a point. He made his point and influenced an entire world with his appeal for nonviolence. Helen Keller defied her blindness and deafness with such intensity that she broke a communication barrier which nearly everyone thought was impossible to break; she learned to speak. Her teacher, Anne Sullivan, was about the only person in young Helen's life who thought it was possible. Miss Sullivan was a visionary in more ways than one.

Intensities in gifted children can be a fascinating, scary, delightful, and exhausting phenomenon to observe or to lasso. We know many gifted children who love to argue and will challenge any rule they think is unfair. But that same intensity is what drives many of them to pursue and accomplish things for which they might later be famous.

In fifth grade, Vinnie was the guy on the team of fifth to eighth graders who answered all of the questions correctly in the Knowledge Master Open,[4] a competition done by computer twice a year. When one of his teammates asked him, "How come you know everything?" Vinnie answered, as though the answer was obvious and that every other kid probably did the same thing, "I read the encyclopedia." Note: Vinnie is not the first gifted kid known to enjoy reading a very hefty tome like the encyclopedia or some other large reference book!

It's ironic, but sometimes adding extra work adds the extra challenge that kids need to keep them motivated to do the regular work, to help them to experience the joy of learning, and to realize that work isn't always done for grades. Otto was a mediocre math student, but his teacher sensed that he was far more capable than his grades indicated. So she began giving him more work and extra challenges instead of making the work easier, and he discovered that he was quite good with math and numbers. He actually *enjoyed* them. She found a way to channel his natural tendency for intensity into a means of increasing his knowledge and productiveness in math. Otto also realized that the extra attention his teacher gave him meant that his efforts and his abilities mattered.

Mrs. McGillicuddy had a zoo room in one of the rural schools she worked at. They had a lobster, an octopus, sea horses, sea anemones, a pregnant guinea pig, a snake, lovebirds, a cockatiel, rabbits, anoles, spiders, and a frog—just to mention a few. The kids loved it. They even had three generations of doves, which they cared for and watched and studied. Eight-year-old Jeff grew to love the animals so much that he decided he wasn't going to eat any more meat. He told his mom, "No more!" But he still ate hamburgers. He simply didn't realize where hamburgers came from. One day, his older brother, Sam, was giving him a hard time about his beliefs. Sam asked, "Well, if you don't believe in hurting animals and eating their meat, then how come you're eating that hamburger?"

Jeff answered, "It isn't meat from an animal. It's a hamburger!"

So of course, Jeff's helpful big brother then proceeded to tell him, in great detail, where hamburger came from. Whereupon Jeffrey took his hamburger, put it down, and refused to ever eat hamburger again. His mom was furious with Sam, as hamburger was the only significant protein she'd been able to get the kid to eat for months, and now she was going to have to search for new sources.

Not every child reacts to such an extreme, but gifted youngsters can definitely make any subject important by their intense focus on it. Max took up running in high school, not as part of the cross country team or as a weight loss program, but simply as something to do and as a way to get exercise. How much does he run a day? He doesn't keep track. He says he runs until he gets tired or sick (or rather, is about to get sick) because that's how he knows he has reached his limit. That is how Max stretches himself—he looks for and tests his limits.

During her first year of downhill skiing lessons at age 10, Tandi made it to the racing team after just five lessons! With intensity as her fuel, she was soon ski jumping competitively.

Gregory, one of Tamara's students, is a great example of intensity. He throws himself wholeheartedly into everything he does. In first grade, while working on a creative thinking activity, he sang, quite expressively, the song "Hakuna Matata" from *The Lion King*, word for word, beginning to end. After finishing the song, he then threw himself into a fairly heated theology debate with Jay, who was only in kindergarten that year. They bantered back and forth about whether or not there was a God, and if there was, what He could and could not do. They pressed each other for evidence and ideas. They argued the finer points of belief and faith for probably 15 minutes. Tamara couldn't believe what she was hearing. These boys were only six and seven years old, and they were passionately discussing the topic by posing really thought-provoking questions! On top of it all, they were so intensely involved in their little debate that the bell ringing and other students milling through the room couldn't pierce their bubble. She ushered them toward the door, and they continued their discussion as they made their way back down the hall to their regular classrooms.

We should note here that intensity in gifted children doesn't always have rosy outcomes. In fact, sometimes the results are rather less than appealing. One of Tamara's former students used to scream and cry with such intensity as a toddler that she would literally cause herself to pass out. Sounds like Helen Keller all over again, doesn't it? It's interesting, however, that the same intensity that fueled Helen's tantrums also fueled her positive progress, once the intensity was channeled in a different direction.

Gifted students (and even adults) often hear people tell them that they are "too much" of something—too involved, too emotional, too hyperactive, too curious, too sensitive, too smart for their own good, too weird, and just plain too intense. They must sometimes feel like champion racecar driver Mario Andretti when he said, "If you feel like you are under control, you're just not going fast enough."

Grant was a second-grade student whose mind, body, and mouth seemed to be constantly moving at warp speed. His fervent shouts to answer questions in class were quickly becoming a problem for his teacher and the rest of the class. The problem wasn't that he was excited about learning—he was. The problem wasn't that he always had the correct answer—he did. No, what concerned his teacher was the bad manners he was showing by not raising his hand. Raising hands in classrooms is like driving on the right side of the road. When everyone does it, things go a lot more smoothly for all involved. His perceptive teacher recognized that he just needed a voice. He was intent on being heard, and with so many other children around competing for the teacher's attention, by golly he had just set his mind to be sure he could express himself.

Since her goal for him was to help him learn to raise his hand, this teacher established something called a progressive contract with him where, for the first level, he had to raise his hand, even if he still shouted out the answer. Just getting him to stick his hand in the air before talking was actually a big step in the right direction! Once he got used to having his hand up before/while talking, she then moved him on to the next level of the contract, waiting to be called on before answering. For a time, this meant that he was often the first student she called on in a discussion because he wasn't yet patient enough to let someone else go first. This wasn't favoritism; it was that little carrot hanging out in front of the donkey. That he was raising his hand and waiting long enough to be the first student called on was progress for him! The other students were so relieved that he wasn't shouting out anymore that they didn't mind that he was still first. Gradually, the teacher moved him to being the second student called on, and then the third, and after awhile, he really had the hang of the routine. His reward? He learned how to manage his intensity.

Catherine, another former student of Tamara's, is another example of over-the-top intensity. It seems that throughout her entire life, Catherine has intensely and completely immersed herself into various topics for approximately two weeks at a time. She will learn everything she can about the topic in a two-week cram session, which means she will literally eat, breathe, dress, talk, think, and even write and spell with the topic as her theme. Total immersion. Before entering school, most of Catherine's two-week obsessions were characters from her own imagination, including one she called "Humphrey Bat," complete with a special cape and hat. While in the persona of Humphrey Bat, Catherine even tried sleeping hanging upside-down from the bar in her closet. Catherine was four when her little sister, Maria, was born. Elephants were her interest (or obsession) at that point. The story goes that she visited her new baby sister in the hospital for the first time wearing an elephant costume. When a man entered the elevator with her and her dad, Catherine said, "Don't worry, sir, I'm not a real elephant."

In first grade, her two-week intense rabbit obsession transformed Catherine into "Super Bunny," with cape, bunny ears, and all. She even wore them to school, much to the consternation of her mother and her teachers. Completing the picture, she insisted that sauerkraut was her kryptonite!

Later, Catherine's two-week obsessions took on the flavor of historical figures, movies, or topics she was studying in school. In her Edgar Allen Poe period, she read all of his works within two weeks and wrote pieces with a similarly dark and poetic flavor. When "Episode One" from the *Star Wars*™ series came out, she stayed up all night for days on end watching and re-watching the *Star Wars*™ movies and came to school dressed as Princess Leia. Later, a simple English project on Joan of Arc spurred her to fashion some armor, create yet another cape, and live the role beyond the assignment—and beyond the walls of that classroom.

Today, Catherine has grown up and gone off to college—an Ivy League college—where she continues to have two-week passions. A Cold War class inspired her to design and wear the costume of a Communist insurgent, complete with Soviet army boots and even a plastic AK-47. An orange portion on the gun helped wide-mouthed gawkers know it wasn't real. One of her professors commented, "What is this, Catherine? You're adding props to your costumes?" It wasn't the first time she had costumed-up at college, and it was just freshman year! By senior year, she had been voted the "Most Recognizable Person on Campus" by her peers. Is it any wonder why?

Maria, Catherine's sister, is another excellent example of intensity, though in a more long-term fashion rather than in two-week spurts. During her freshman year of high school, Maria read *all* of Shakespeare's works, including the lesser-known "Non-Dramatic Poems" and "Troilius and Cressida." Talk about intellectual intensity. As a young girl, she came across a set of books about "Women in History," which she read and re-read until they literally fell apart from the wear and tear. Her real love, though, is science. Science is her oxygen. Her family reports that when pursuing an experiment at home, Maria (a junior in high school) will forego food and sleep for hours and even, yes, days. She says that testing a hypothesis is like releasing a precious part of her soul upon the world, placing it before the mercy of "science" and "truth." Summers and weeklong school holidays find her in her homemade laboratory in the basement of her house doing Western Blotting[5] experiments or examining specimens under the microscope. Because Western Blotting requires long periods of care and observation, it's not uncommon for Maria to go without food and sleep for 24 to 72 hours during these intense forays into research.

It would be easy for someone on the "outside" to say that Maria's focus during these times is unhealthy or absurd. But wait. Remember the Wright brothers? Their discovery had a pretty important impact on travel and transportation. And it took them some intense periods of time and focus to accomplish what they were after.

Einstein focused so intently while working on physics problems that he became unaware of the world around him. Marie Curie frequently missed meals and went without sleeping while studying or experimenting because she would lose track of time or because the experiment warranted attention. Where would we be without the contributions from these intense individuals? Did you have passionate interests when you were a child? Did you have dreams of being a scientist or mathematician? These early passions are important. They help shape our future lives. Here are some words from a former gifted student (now an adult) who had an early passion for anatomy:

> *Back in fifth grade, I decided I wanted to be a cardiothoracic surgeon when I grew up. It was my first sheep's heart dissection that did it for me. I thought it was so cool getting to hold and investigate and mess with something that used to be inside an animal's body, helping it live, and thought that since the sight of blood and something's internal organs didn't gross me out like it did the other kids, that must mean something. After that, I took some dissection and anatomy*

courses offered through the elementary school's GT
program (the school district was affluent there,
though I wasn't. I got lucky because the parsonage
of the church my dad was serving in was on the
right side of the district division line—and ahead
of its time), and basically every school project for
years thereafter was about the heart. I even
brought in a bucket of sheep organs (bought by my
dear mom from the butcher for 34 cents—a heart,
a diaphragm, two lungs, and the trachea!) to do a
demo dissection for a class project in seventh grade.
I still sort of pride myself in having made a girl I
didn't like throw up.

How fortunate for this student that she had supportive
teachers as well as a mother who not only allowed her to pursue
her interests, but actually encouraged it! In this particular case,
the student did not grow up to be a cardiothoracic surgeon,
though she is pursuing a graduate degree in the field of International Public Health.

Catherine and Maria are lucky to have an understanding
mother, too. But every mother has her limits! And this mother
was also one who knew when it was time to say, "Enough." The
previous owners of their home had apparently been poachers
who'd gotten caught. No wonder the house had been sold for so
little money! Before allegedly skipping town to Canada, the
poachers buried a grizzly bear carcass in the garden in the backyard, a fact (yes, an apparent and unfortunate fact) that they
mentioned to the home's new owners. Years later, when
Catherine was six, her mom made the fateful mistake of mentioning the bear to her. Well, news of buried bio-treasure is
clearly a neon sign of opportunity to a curious child!

Catherine soon had her neighborhood friends organized
into digging teams, and the excavation began. They worked
intently for a whole week, digging two at a time in shifts, and

gradually a hole grew in the garden that was large enough and deep enough to fit three kids at the same time all the way down inside of it. Amazing!

Meanwhile, a patient mother waited for them to lose interest (or wear out) before she began her gardening for the year. Unfortunately, just about the time she thought they would give up, Catherine discovered a vertebra, which meant the kids were *sure* they were on the verge of finding the skull!

Now, gardening in Montana presents a small planting window, and that window would soon be closed. Catherine's mom announced her plans to bring in the rototiller in a few days. To the kids, rototilling their "dig" could prevent the Archaeological Breakthrough of the Century! Instantly, Catherine began organizing her friends, and even three-year-old Maria, into a protest, complete with picket signs. Forming a little human chain around the hole itself, they marched and chanted, waving the signs they had made: "Unfair!" "Save our hole! It can't go!"

Intensity! What was Catherine's mom to do?

Although she saw that the kids were serious about this, she told the rototiller man to go ahead and put the rototiller into the garden. When he started it up, it made such a loud and terrible noise that it scared all of the kids and sent them running and screaming from their hole, picket signs flying behind.

Put that on your list of teaching maxims: *When intensity threatens to override common sense, start up a rototiller and watch them run—buwahaha!*

Seriously. Though it is often seen and misunderstood as weird, crazy, and "abnormal behavior," the intensity of gifted children (and adults) is of keen importance to their abilities and accomplishments. Going against the flow, ignoring naysayers and critics, thinking innovatively and divergently, and pursuing one's talents and interests with a passion that belies all normalcy—these are the vehicle, while intensity is the fuel.

And an astute and supportive teacher can sometimes step in and help with the steering. Anne Sullivan was able to do this for

Helen Keller. Helen Keller writes in *The Story of My Life,* "I took the book in my hands and tried to feel the letters with an intensity of longing that I can never forget." Helen was born with natural passions and intensities. Anne Sullivan took this child, whose intensity was first expressed in the form of tantrums and frustrations, and taught her how to channel that same intensity of feeling into learning and later into productive pursuits. Helen Keller didn't just rise to the challenge of her disabilities, she did more; through her intense passions, she excelled and passed up most of her peers, disabled or otherwise, along the way.

When you find yourself overwhelmed by the intensity of someone in your life, think about Helen, Maria, Catherine, Jeff, Vinnie, and Orville and Wilbur. Although a little channeling and polish may be in order from time to time, try to remember that it is that inborn intensity of gifted individuals which often spurs on the progress and new discoveries that enlighten our world.

If only these folks could bottle it up for the rest of us!

4: Asynchrony

Asynchronous development is a key characteristic of gifted children, and many experts in the field even define giftedness with the use of the term.

It's easy to notice the exceptionalities of gifted children if you know what to look for. Gifted children stand out. Because they talk early, read early, and multiply early, others usually notice. Adults wonder, "hmmmm," and the lightbulb goes on. We think to ourselves, "Something's up with this kid."

Sometimes parents don't notice anything unusual until their child starts school, especially if the child isn't spending much time with other children her age, or if she is in an environment where she is with other children who are gifted like she is. In this case, the child seems perfectly "normal" or "average" because the parents have been with her since birth and don't see that she is at all unusual. But once the child enters school or a situation where she is with other children, the differences are more apparent. For example, Karen's son Stanley was reading at two years. At first, this *did* seem a little unusual for a toddler, but after some time, it seemed normal. And while it *did* clue her in to her child's exceptional abilities in some areas, other areas weren't so apparent, as they were overshadowed by the reading and comprehension skills until Stanley began kindergarten and his skills could be compared to those of the average kindergarten student. His lack of skills in other areas also seemed normal until compared to the rest of the class. Karen was surprised to see how physically coordinated the other students were when compared to Stanley. This may be a good thing to keep in mind. Some parents just don't realize that their children are different and may have different needs in the classroom.

Kindergarten teachers may run into some of these unusual children. When conducting her beginning-of-the-year student assessments, Wilson's kindergarten teacher asked him if he could count to 100. He confidently replied, "Would you like it in English or Spanish?" And he could have done either one.

Because gifted children seem to develop in some areas well ahead of other children their same age, we say that their development is asynchronous, or "out of sync." Their development is out of step—not just with the world around them, but within themselves as well. For example, the gifted six-year-old above might be able to do counting or addition or even multiplication like a nine-year-old, but he might cry like any other six-year-old when his feelings get hurt. He also might be able to hold his own in a Saturday chess game with his father but would then go out to play "fort" in his backyard treehouse with his neighborhood friends. There is nothing wrong with him. His intellectual development is just ahead of his physical and social/emotional development. It happens all of the time with gifted children. It's one of the things we learn to watch for. We also need to be sure we don't expect a six-year-old gifted child to act at all times like a nine-year-old, even though that may be his intellectual level. He is still a six-year-old, but one who is advanced in some areas.

Sometimes gifted children may lag behind their age peers in certain areas, too. According to her mother, Tyla didn't begin talking until she was four years old. Not a peep before then! Yet now she's in the gifted program and is doing very well. Is Tyla alone in this distinction? Not at all. Albert Einstein didn't talk until he was three or four years old either, yet as an adult, he was able to effectively communicate about one of the most complex scientific theories in the history of the world. We're so used to gifted children being ahead of the game intellectually (and sometimes in other areas, too) that we forget they're still kids. But that's important to remember, because it's when we forget that they're still kids that we find ourselves frustrated with what would otherwise be considered normal behavior.

Vijay is a 13-year-old with a passionate desire to know everything about sea turtles. He raises money for sea turtle preservation funds and educates other students about them. He wins spelling bees, excels in math and science, and uses a vocabulary that prompts many adults to ask, "What does that mean?" But Vijay is still a kid. Sometimes he chews on the end of his sleeve in class, leaving holes and tatters and soggy wetness as telltale signs. Sometimes he trips over his own feet while walking down the hall. He forgets his notebook most days. "Absent-minded professor" comes to mind. As his teacher, it could be easy to get frustrated with him and wonder "what his problem is." You've probably asked yourself a similar question about a youngster you know: "If he's so smart, then how come…?" If he can distinguish the minute differences between certain sea turtle species, then why can't he remember to bring his notebook to class?

And why does a six-year-old with an extensive adult vocabulary and comprehension use this gift to describe his unrealistic fantasyland where he leads an army of ninjas?[6] The reason is his asynchronous development. Mix adult language skills with young boy imagination and you have a certain asynchrony.

And frankly, tripping over one's feet once in a while and forgetting one's notebook every few days are pretty normal things for 13-year-old boys.

When Tyrell was in the second grade, he hung out with all of the older kids because he could relate better to them. They were his early role models, and they were closer to his intellectual level.

(Older and mixed-age friends are very common with gifted kids, by the way.) In second grade, Tyrell was creating his own elaborate mazes, "choose your own adventure" stories, and imaginative worlds. He examined bugs out on the playground and used his free time to learn about ocean life. It was also in second grade that Tyrell one day poured a whole bottle of glue into an empty desk for no real reason other than perhaps boredom. He neglected to first consider the possible result. Realizing after the fact (when it had dried to a fairly hard lump) that it probably wasn't such a good idea, he used a pair of classroom scissors to try to scrape it out. When the scissors bent, he grabbed another pair. When that pair bent, he got another pair. Almost before he realized it, he'd ruined almost an entire classroom set of scissors! Not to mention the scratched-up, gooey desk. Needless to say, his mom and teacher weren't too pleased! How could this kid who was otherwise so on-the-ball do something so irrational and juvenile?

Here's your answer again: asynchrony.

Doesn't that sound like just the sort of thing a first or second grader would do?

His judgment matches his age. But for many intellectual things, he is advanced and prefers older playmates.

There are times when it is important to acknowledge exceptional intellectual abilities and encourage their cultivation and potential, but there are also times when, darn it, these are kids, and we need to acknowledge that as well. Not only that, but we need to *appreciate* the delightful contrasts, the innocence and the maturing process, the freshness of new brains as they comprehend and react to their world on every level.

A gifted child came home from kindergarten, jubilant, one day. "Mommy," she said, "Do you know what happens when someone has a birthday? The Prince comes out of his office and gives you a pencil and a birthday card!" A royal principal-administrator indeed. School is a magical, fairy-tale kind of place for her. Let her have her illusions. Later that same year, the principal unknowingly re-enforced his royal status when he dressed up as a knight for Halloween and rode a real horse onto the playground in front of all of the kids. We'll bet any five-year-old would agree that this was magical—including the gifted ones.

There are two sayings that are often repeated by teachers who work with gifted children: (1) They are children first, and they are gifted second; and (2) They are always more than their test scores. We are dealing with children *and* their abilities, which are in many ways inseparable, but the child part has to come first.

One of the things gifted kids often enjoy is using their imaginations. They have the ability to be logical, rational, concise, and literal, but they also love that fantasy world and long to spend time there as well. Their imaginations and their youth allow them that privilege. We should, too. There will be plenty of time for them to grow and mature and become well-rounded people.

Kindergarteners and first graders enter the classroom from every direction. Their sweet innocence sneaks up on us and reminds us that they're still kids. They come from every culture, every religion, and every standard of living. They come from big families where they have to fight for the last piece of dessert, and they come from small families where they get the entire cheesecake all to themselves. They have one parent or two, and sometimes more than two. They can live under strict rules or none at all or somewhere in between. Combine this with their individual personalities and mix it up in a new-to-them classroom. The teacher's job is to take this mix, and with it the potential for chaos, and organize it.

You have our sympathies.

One kindergarten teacher decided to have a banquet where the children were in charge of setting the table. It was an important lesson, not because she was training future waiters, waitresses, or Martha Stewarts, but because, believe it or not, one of her students didn't know what eating utensils were used for. Does this imply that this particular child was lacking in brain potential? No, it simply means that the child had little or no experience in that area. She was asynchronous compared to most children her age when it came to eating utensils. Her parents had somehow managed to shelter her from the evils of knives, forks, and chopsticks.

The thing is, children don't come to class having read the instructions on how to behave or what society expects from them, or even what you expect from them. No matter what their intellectual capabilities are, their knowledge is based on their experiences. They still innocently believe that everyone lives the way they do at their house.

Another new kid came in to the class in the middle of the year. As children his age often do, he found himself desperately in need of the restroom, as he had waited until the very last minute. So his sympathetic teacher gave him the big wooden key that he was supposed to wear around his neck as a hall pass. About 10 minutes later, this little boy came back sobbing and holding himself. "Teacher, the key won't fit!" The poor kid had tried using the big wooden key to unlock the stall door, which some other thoughtful little boy had latched from the inside before he crawled out under the door.

Think about it. We're willing to bet that most of those children, as varied as their lives may have been before they entered that school building, probably shared the common experience that keys were used for unlocking things, not as a permission pass for walking in hallways.

Because little kids also don't have the experience that results in adult judgment, Show and Tell or examples from home can sometimes be a scary place to venture. Discretion may be the better part of valor, but in the brain of a five- or six-year-old, it simply doesn't exist.

Once, Mr. Jackson, the art teacher, was explaining symmetry to the first grade class and used his finger to draw a line down the middle of his face, saying, "Look. My face is symmetrical. I have one eye and one eye; and one ear and one ear...." Then one of his students, Bella, raised her hand and said innocently, "My butt cheeks are symmetrical."

Uh huh. A perfect example of gifted, out-of-the-box thinking combined with inexperience and innocence.

Young kids have no qualms about telling the entire class anything and everything they could want to know about their families' personal lives either. These are not necessarily appropriate topics for classroom discussion at that age, but almost inevitably, some will be mentioned. Also inevitably, the rest of the class will be fascinated and will have oodles of questions for the lucky celebrity.

Side note to parents: Don't kid yourself thinking that your child doesn't have any embarrassing stories to tell. These kids are sharp. They know what makes a good story, and they're always on the lookout for it. They have no qualms about announcing to the class that mom had a rather gassy evening the night before or that dad walks around in his boxers at home.

Yes, savvy parents have Show and Tell day marked on their calendars—in big red letters.

Teachers are the lucky ones who get to hear all of the exciting stuff and monitor the discussions. We can just imagine how the journal entries of a kindergarten teacher might read:

> *Johnny announced to the class today that his mother can't eat too many fruits and vegetables or she sounds like a foghorn, but she always makes him eat his fruits and vegetables. He wishes he could sound like a foghorn. Note to self: Try not to giggle when I see Johnny's mother next week at parent/teacher conference.*

We can also imagine that there might be several parents who would pay that teacher good money to hand over her secret journal and forget what she knows. Hint to teachers: This might be a great idea for a retirement plan.

Another highly gifted seven-year-old boy was watching the news on TV one night when he saw the parents of one of the boys in his class get arrested for doing what seemed to be a science project. By the time his own parents came home, he was in a panic, thinking that the world had gone crazy arresting people for science projects. After all, his own brother and sister had done science fair projects in the past, and his parents had been accessories to the crimes.

The boy's dad asked him, "Did the science project on the news happen to involve a lab?"

"Yeah! The police said they found a lab in their basement!"

This answer was followed by a little discussion on the legality questions and differences involved in science projects and chemicals used for drug production. It's a fine line.

Kids, even the highly gifted, are innocent and naïve in many areas. They lack world experience. Sometimes this is one of their greatest charms. This is what we *want* from them. Although *some* of those charms are better enjoyed after the fact. Here are a couple of examples.

> Madelyne and her mother had the following conversation when she was barely three years old:
>
> Mom: If you had three apples and I gave you two more, how many would you have?
>
> Madelyne: Five!
>
> Mom: If you had two grapes and I gave you one more, how many would you have?
>
> Madelyne: Three!
>
> After a brief pause, Madelyne commented, "If I had two pieces of cheese and one glass of water, then I'd be all full!"

A couple of years later, at the ripe old age of five, this same child asked, "What's 'skratchety'?"

Mom answered, "I don't know what you're talking about."

After thinking a moment, Madelyne piped up, "Oh, I remember—it means 'plan of attack.'" She meant "strategy." Gifted children love language and new skills and concepts and can hardly wait to use them. As Karen's six-year-old son Rupert says when he uses a large word incorrectly and is told by a sibling that he doesn't know what he means, "I know. I just like to use it."

One summer a number of years ago, a teacher was visiting the public library when she was approached by Jill, one of Tamara's students who, at age seven, had just finished second grade. "Hi, Mrs. Lopez. I'm trying to learn about American history because I'm writing historical fiction now. Do you know if the speech that starts with 'Our fathers, brought forth on this continent, a new nation...' is from the Preamble to the Constitution? Or was it Lincoln's Gettysburg Address?"

After picking her jaw up off the floor, Mrs. Lopez helped Jill use the card catalog to find the resources she needed. Is it possible some of us are checking our own memories right now for the source of that quotation??!!

With examples like these of how gifted kids stand out with their asynchrony, it's easy to see how the adults can begin to assume they are dealing with a miniature adult. But for their own sanity, it's wise for them to remember that they are dealing with a child.

Asynchrony can be charming, but it can also be frustrating, not only for those around them who never know which side of the child/adult brain they're going to see, but for the kids themselves. It's frustrating when your age peers don't get your jokes or want to play your games or don't care about the latest bits of trivia that you carefully gleaned from the encyclopedia last night. It's also frustrating when people expect more of you that you are able to give.

The good news is that although they may be out-of-sync with most of their age peers, gifted kids find they are in sync with their intellectual peers. Like little orbiting magnets, they somehow gravitate toward one another. They share similar interests and communicate in similar ways. They can commiserate with one another about their common challenges.

It's helpful to realize that thanks to their asynchrony, gifted children may require more than one set of peers. They require both intellectual peers who can hold their own in a conversation about history or genetic mutations, and age peers who are at a similar maturity level for certain other activities, maybe playing backyard tag.

If they are asked, gifted students will often talk of being academically out of step with their classmates and how this creates obstacles for them. Very early on, they set long-term, lofty goals and actually work toward them.

In first grade, number one on Aleesha's priority list was getting her homework done. She knew she'd be heading off to college someday, and in her six-year-old mind, getting her first-grade homework done was an important step on that journey. The future-oriented planning and foresight of a gifted child can be both astonishing and unnerving. They can make the connections between how "the little things" turn into "the big things." In high school, when their classmates are more concerned with senior ditch day or who's dating whom, some gifted kids are researching in their basement laboratories, composing music, reading Dostoyevsky, or painting a 40 square-foot masterpiece on the kitchen wall.

Weird? Well, yes. But weird could be a compliment. It indicates asynchrony again. And if we peek through a yearbook of history at those who've made significant positive contributions to society, we'll find quite a few out-of-sync alums.

If he had been older than first grade at the time, Ole's classmates probably would've called him weird because of the business he started that year. Talk about enterprising. And forethought. He convinced his parents to buy a few cases of licorices in various flavors, then he talked with the principal about getting a "business license" to sell his product in the school hallway. He blitzed the halls with advertising, then came to school and set up shop—selling licorice out of his briefcase! He made a killing. Pretty good for a first grader, no?

We know these kids are precocious and asynchronous. Are they so different they're a little bit "weird"? Einstein once made the comment: "A question that sometimes drives me hazy: am I or are the others crazy?" Einstein himself wasn't exactly well-rounded. Thank goodness! "Well-rounded" is fine and dandy, but this world also needs a few people who shoot off in one direction, who fail in some areas because all of their energy is spent developing another area of their specialty.

Gifted children may fall behind in one area while they zoom ahead in another. They need to know it's okay to be out of sync. After all, "gifted" doesn't mean a person has to be exceptional at *everything*.

Let's take Nikola Tesla.[7] You may not know his name. He wasn't the guy to bring the world an early version of *Forbes Magazine*, nor was he particularly adept at social skills, but he did have plenty of other highly developed and highly useful talents that we all benefit from today. Sometimes called the "Forgotten Father of Technology" or "the man who invented the 20th Century," Tesla had 113 patents. His complex mind allowed him a most unusual method of inventing. He would literally imagine and create in his mind every detail, every accurate measurement, and every working part of one of his inventions before trying to put it into concrete form. In dozens of cases, he never even put pencil to paper; he simply told the machinists the measurements and they could create his invention. And each time it turned out correctly on the first try!

Born in Serbia, Tesla followed opportunities in his homeland and then in America and Canada. He was fluent in seven languages, and he had the ability to memorize entire texts. Though they were mostly rivals, he worked with Thomas Edison. He designed the mechanism that captured hydroelectric power from Niagara Falls (alternating current), and a series of his patents formed the basis of today's electric power systems, bringing Edison's light to the masses of the world. In spite of his rare genius, he was also a deplorable accountant who went bankrupt more than once. He was strange in his friendships. He preferred the company of pigeons to that of other people, although he did have a small handful of friends (including Mark Twain). He was compulsive and obsessive and may very likely have been given the label of OCD (Obsessive Compulsive Disorder) in his later years. What an array of wide-ranging talents and experiences, eh? It seems Nikola Tesla was one guy who rode through life on the roller coaster of asynchrony.

Being gifted is rarely a perfectly balanced brain position. It can send abilities, passions, and strengths surging in one direction while other aspects of a child's personality and skills remain underdeveloped—or at least they appear that way when compared with their talents. In fact, they may be developing at a perfectly normal pace for a child that age.

Though the clichés abound (*our children are our greatest natural resource, our children are the future*, etc., etc.), these clichés really are true. Before we saddle the hopes of the world on the small shoulders of our gifted youth, however, we might be wise to remember—talents and futures notwithstanding—that they're also still just young people who laugh and giggle, suck their thumbs, trip over their shoelaces, forget their homework, pine for a boyfriend or girlfriend, now and then receive failing grades, don't comprehend certain subjects as well as others, and sometimes make dumb and irrational choices just like any other kid. While we shouldn't deny them their intellect and appropriate matching opportunities, neither should we deny them their childhood and the opportunities to be "just kids."

Gifted children require adults who will allow them an opportunity to mature socially, emotionally, and physically at an average pace, even while their brains are racing ahead to embrace complex ideas beyond their years. They need adults who can meet their needs at either end, who can both separate the child from the brain and yet help them become whole, all at the same time. They need acceptance of who they are at any given moment, and emotional support and encouragement to grow into the person they will become. Understanding asynchrony makes acceptance easier.

5: Attention to Detail

"I never ran my train off the track, and I never lost a passenger."
~ Harriet Tubman ~

Attention to detail and desire for accuracy are always among the lists detailing the characteristics common to gifted children. People who are gifted possess these traits because their intellectual capacity creates in them the ability to see and reach for a higher level of precision. These traits are also seen in people we call perfectionists, and they may often be noticed in gifted students through their use of language. They will frequently use clarifying words and phrases such as "actually," "technically," "it depends on," "specifically," "in theory," "essentially," "in reality," or "to be more precise."

Tamara noticed this need for precision a few years ago when her sixth graders were working on a design project in class. As they were putting their ideas down on graph paper using pencils and rulers, three of the boys were discussing their individual ideas amongst themselves. Tamara didn't mind that they were conferring. The problem was that they were doing so at the tops of their voices (not all that unusual for 12-year-old boys!), and their volume was distracting to the other students.

Tamara said, "Fellas, you're only sitting two feet away from each other; you don't need to be talking so loudly!"

Before she could say another word, they had whisked their rulers out and laid them end-to-end between them. "Actually,

Miss Fisher, we're only 19 inches apart." It's typical of gifted kids. They like to challenge us. And yes, accuracy is everything to them.

Just a kindergartner, Wendell provides another example. Tamara asked him, "How high can you count?"

"Well," he said, "technically, I can count to 1,000, but it would take me awhile." Kindergarten, mind you.

Another example is Amanda. When she was four, she would get very frustrated if she accidentally colored with her crayon outside of the lines of the coloring book pictures. Today, as a 10-year-old, if anything is new or out of place in her home, she notices immediately. Nothing gets past her. She observes every detail.

So how important is this attention to detail? And perfectionism? If you need double-bypass surgery, do you want your surgeon to have concern for detail? How about your accountant? Do you hire the one who overlooks important small things or the one who knows the relevance of all of the details in tax law? Let's face it, details count! Especially in certain situations or circumstances.

Harriet Tubman[8] fled from Maryland to Pennsylvania in 1849 in search of her freedom. But it wasn't enough for her to be free. She wanted *all* slaves to be free. Over the next 10 years, she repeatedly risked her life to win freedom for a few hundred others. Could she rely on luck and a lackadaisical attitude? If she had, she wouldn't have been nearly so successful. Harriet was well-known for her highly detailed plans and for taking into account all possible obstacles. She was prepared for *anything*. For example, when scouting out routes ahead of her group, she would carry two chickens with her. If she thought that anyone was getting suspicious of her wanderings, she would release the chickens and chase them around, pretending they were loose and she was trying to catch them. Suspicions would soon be alleviated, because how could this ineffective chicken-chaser be up to anything?

Harriet Tubman's focus on the details of any possible situation allowed her to successfully tackle each of the challenges that came her way. Her freedom-seeking charges knew that she was highly focused on their safe travel. She was even willing to attend to one detail that showed she was even aware that danger could come from within. The pistol she packed was not only to defend against slave catchers, but also to threaten and even shoot any runaway slave who might chicken out and turn back. She couldn't risk her secrets being exposed or "beaten out" of a returning runaway. Down to this last, thorny detail, she had planned for everything. She told her charges, "You'll be free or die."

How's that for an example of extreme perfectionism? And yet, would anything less have been so successful? Perfectionism, and attention to detail in this case, was required.

Harriet didn't personally lead all of the slaves she rescued to freedom. Most of them, as a matter of fact, got to safety based solely on her detailed descriptions of the route to take. Without being able to write it all down, imagine the care she had to take to be sure they understood and remembered exactly what she was telling them. This Moses of her people knew that the details mattered if freedom was to be achieved.

No pressure or anything, Harriet. All this world will require of you will be a whole lot of courage and an extra-heavy dose of perfectionism.

Sometimes perfectionism is healthy and necessary. Sometimes it isn't.

Healthy perfectionism involves an understanding of when details are important, as well as a willingness to make the effort to achieve an appropriate level of excellence. Unhealthy perfectionism involves a desperate desire to be perfect in all things, even when being perfect is not important, since any mistake is considered a defect. Unhealthy perfection can lead to ulcers, a fear of taking positive risks, and a fear of failing. Essentially, as psychologist Maureen Neihart points out, perfectionism is like cholesterol: there's a good kind and bad kind. Caring adults can help children understand both kinds of perfectionism and also know when they can let up on the pressure they put on themselves.

Some gifted children concern themselves so much with the little things—with the trimmings—that they never get to the meat of the assignment. Roberto spends so much time on the numbering of his list of spelling words—making sure each number is aligned perfectly with the number above it—that he may not finish his spelling test. Lucy gets so caught up in writing her essay perfectly that she never actually finishes it. She begins, decides that her topic isn't exactly right, spends hours stressing over it, finally settles on a new one, then doesn't like the beginning sentence of her first paragraph, and can't go on with the rest of it until she perfects that sentence. Finally, she is so frustrated that she doesn't complete the assignment. She may conclude she's no good at essays only because she can't meet her own unrealistic expectations. She won't invest her time in improving her skills because she doesn't see the point of it. She tells herself that she simply can't write essays.

LaVonne, on the other hand, may approach his essay differently. He may ponder over each word in a painstaking effort to achieve his best. If he's happy with his final product, if he's not developing ulcers, and if his perfectionism doesn't take over his life and inhibit his choices, then he's doing just fine. It's all right to have a desire to achieve excellence in a certain area or on a particular project. We really *do* need people who are willing to work that hard. The challenge is to keep the perfectionism in a healthy realm and not let it permeate every single activity.

Gifted children who strive for accurate details usually show signs of this trait at a very young age. When Melanie was two and three years old, she would stack and re-stack a pile of blocks until she had them just so. Unlike most toddlers with short attention spans, she was able to focus on this task for hours until she was satisfied. When Cameron was five, he had a tree fort that was accessible only by climbing a rope. While part of his time up there was spent in imaginative play (fighting off the barbarians and talking like a weasel), most of his time there was devoted to cleaning out every single pine needle from his little haven. He loved to clean, and it was an enjoyable form of play for him to focus on banishing those pesky needles.

Raymund loved to play with Legos® and couldn't be satisfied with a construction he had built unless it was perfectly symmetrical, meaning the same colors and number of pieces appeared in the same locations on both sides. And if the right piece wasn't there, he'd find a way to make it work so that at least the outside looked symmetrical, even if the inside didn't.

In fifth grade, Carrie got a B+ on her report card. That's a great grade, and although she knew that, she also had her eyes on a bigger prize—Law School. Carrie knew when she was still very young that she wanted to be an attorney someday. She also knew that good grades would help her get there, so she was determined not to let this one B+ in fifth grade stand in her way! Not knowing that law schools never check fifth-grade report cards, and unbeknownst to her parents, Carrie called her principal at home and argued her case (like any good lawyer) for an A-. She got it, too. Now that's the kind of lawyer I want working for me! Detail-oriented, persistent, and gutsy! That was 15 years ago. Guess what she's up to nowadays? She's a lawyer!

Eric's mother says he can take a 15-minute assignment and turn it into a 45-minute project. True, some projects and assignments are worth a little extra effort, but Eric's mother believes he would be a lot happier if he could tell when an assignment is worth the stress and extra effort and when it isn't. Gifted children sometimes take the old adage "Anything worth doing is worth doing well" to the extreme. It's good to tie your shoes in a decent knot, sure, but if you can't get out the door and you miss the bus regularly because the laces aren't hanging down at exactly the same length, you might want to rethink your priorities. Fix the laces *after* you are safely on the bus. Let things slide now and then. When one can do so, when one knows the difference between excellence and perfection, when one can accept something a little less than excellence on things that truly don't matter, then it's healthy perfectionism.

Remember the precision we talked about earlier? A gifted child is usually the one who will ask a teacher for clarification. If the teacher says the assignment is due by Tuesday, the gifted child will be the one asking, "Do you mean before Tuesday, or do you mean by the beginning of school on Tuesday, or do you mean by the end of school on Tuesday?" They force the rest of us into improved accuracy.

When they are older, these same kids can talk about the advantages and disadvantages their perfectionism has brought them. A job well done *matters* to them and feels good. They're disappointed when something is less than it could be. They put their all into what is important to them, and they achieve more because of this. But when taken to an extreme, there are times perfectionism can hold them back. Melanie, for example, didn't try out for the All Northwest Choir because she was afraid of possible failure. She couldn't stand the thought of not making it when she was certain several of the other kids she knew would pass the audition. Even though she probably also would have made it, an uncertain outcome (in other words, no guarantee of success) kept her from trying out and from taking that risk.

Gifted children who are perfectionists can be hard on themselves, too. In their mind's eye, they're able to create elaborate and beautifully polished final products, yet reality doesn't usually hold up to that. Their project or paper is never good enough. They get bogged down in the details and forget that the overall product is often more important. Time and experience help.

In the meantime, how do we help gifted children to prioritize their tasks in order to give them the opportunity to focus on the things that matter the most to them? How do we help them look bravely into the face of fear of failure and imperfection until they can obliterate the power it has over them?

Ha! Good luck. We all live in fear of failure, a little bit anyway. The trick is to help these kids put it in perspective. The best way we can do this is by our own example. As authority figures in front of the classroom, we have to feel comfortable with the idea that we don't know everything, nor do we do everything well. And we're okay with that. We can talk about times we tried something and failed. Talk about the mistakes we made and learned from. Talk about how we can admit when we're wrong and thus avoid a power struggle over who is right.

Let the kids see you make and talk about mistakes. Maybe you could even make some mistakes on purpose. If you're working a math problem on the board and it's a skill that at least some of the kids are pretty familiar with, add the numbers incorrectly, and let them notice and correct you. Then say, "Oops! Good thing you were watching!" Do it a few times here and there, and you'll notice that the kids really *are* watching, more than ever, because they *want* to catch you making mistakes. It's comforting to them to think that they might have a little something of value going on in their brains, that they're competent, and that they can, at times, question the teacher's work. They learn to think for themselves with confidence rather than always relying on outside sources to do their thinking for them. And there's that glorious side benefit—they see you make a mistake, smile, and handle it gracefully. You are modeling—a powerful teaching method. You give them the example so that they can do the same.

Tamara knows a teacher who used a similar strategy every day. Miss Cardwell offered the students one point of extra credit if they caught a mistake somewhere, even in something she, the teacher, had done. Certainly the students had to be polite in calling it to her attention if it was her mistake, but they gleefully brought mistakes to her attention from a variety of surprising sources. Are there sometimes mistakes in your local newspaper? You bet. Have you ever driven by a billboard that had a word misspelled on it or incorrect punctuation? Sometimes books get printed with errors in them! The students from Miss Cardwell's class would actually take pictures of billboards with mistakes on them while they were on vacation and bring them in for verification so they could earn a measly little extra credit point! How cool is that! Of course, they not only had to point out the mistake, they had to know how to correct it to earn the credit.

Could Miss Cardwell have given them a paper and said, "Find the 15 mistakes on this worksheet"? Sure. Would the learning goal have been the same? Yes. Would the learning outcome have been the same? No. The motivation for a worksheet full of purposeful mistakes wouldn't have been nearly as high as it was for a whole world full of accidental mistakes—mistakes that, if they were good enough detectives and knew how to correct them, could earn them a miniscule reward, an extra credit point, and a much bigger reward—satisfaction. Later, that same eye for detail may help them in their careers. Just ask a copy editor or an engineer.

Did the students get bored with this exercise? Nope. The opposite occurred. The students were so happy when they found mistakes in newspapers and on signs that they actually became excited when they found mistakes in their own work because they had learned how easily they could be fixed. Mistakes were *fun* in that classroom!

Sometimes with the overly perfectionistic child—the unhealthy perfectionist—a more straightforward or focused strategy may be needed to help the child realize that while excellence is important, "perfect" is unrealistic. You could have a "Mistakes Fair," the goofs version of Show and Tell, where everyone (including the teacher!) tells a story about a mistake they once made. And follow up with the question, "What did you learn from that experience?" Life often gives the test first and the lesson later. After your Mistakes Fair, you could start a bulletin board where the children (and you) can write about or draw pictures of your mistakes and the lessons you learned from them. Many incredible scientific discoveries came from mistakes, accidents, or failures. Perhaps you could even start a museum of historic mistakes that turned out to be beneficial. Mistakes can be celebrated. We learn from them!

Gifted kids who develop unhealthy levels of perfectionism often do so because not only do *they* want everything they do to be just right, but they strongly believe that everyone else in their lives *expects* them to get everything right, too. We have all been there, grading papers, and along comes little Susie's paper, perfect as always, day after day. And then one day, there's a mistake, and what do we think? "Well, Susie, what was with you that day? How come you got this one wrong? You know how to do this!" The message Susie gets in her mind is that the world around her expects her to be perfect 100% of the time.

Likewise, when little Johnny, who has brought home straight A's since kindergarten, suddenly brings home a B in tenth-grade math, Mom and Dad sometimes focus on the B and why it should've been an A, instead of noting all of the other A's on the report card. Now Johnny is feeling the pressures of unhealthy perfectionism. Did he try his hardest and still only get a B? Pat him on the back! Was he lazy on a few assignments? If his other grades are still A's, then there's hardly an argument for him being lazy overall. We'll wager there's one little piece of your day job you slack on, too—possibly because it's not as important to you. This B could be a really good sign! It could mean that Johnny has finally realized that there are bigger fish to fry in the world than being perfect at everything all of the time.

Imperfection, even when one is trying her best, is often unavoidable. Those of you who know Karen's other book, *Raisin' Brains: Surviving My Smart Family*, will remember the underwear story. Well, one of Tamara's students also had an experience with unmentionables, and it's an experience that illustrates "unavoidable imperfection" to an extreme. Keep in mind that this *is* a true story.

Maria, aside from loving science, also competes on her high school's speech and debate team. One year, just before the semi-final round at the state tournament, Maria noticed that she had a run in her nylon stockings. In the debate between should-I-leave-them-on or should-I-take-them-off, she decided that bare legs were better than a run all the way down her leg. The nylons went in the trash, and Maria soldiered off to take on her competitors in Extemporaneous Speaking. Extemp is a serious speech and debate event in which the students must know a great deal about current events—both national and international. Prompted with a single question and only 30 minutes of preparation time, students have to develop a five- to seven-minute source-based speech that answers the question. Early in her speech, just as she was pointing out why she thought the Federal Reserve was going to soon be raising interest rates by a quarter of a percent, a strange slide of underwear began. The worn elastic had snapped in the waistband of Maria's unmentionables, and she could feel them slowly sliding down. Though adjustments in posture were made, the underwear had soon fallen to her knees. She was wearing a knee-length skirt and managed to catch the offending garment between her knees. They stayed there for a moment, not to be ignored, then boldly slid down to her ankles.

Taking it all in stride, Maria considered her options in her head while still managing to give her speech. Option #1: Sling them over her shoulder and continue the speech. Option #2: Hike them back up while continuing the speech. Though option #1 certainly would've made an impression on the judges, she decided it wasn't quite the right impression. Realizing the judges had probably already gotten to know her a bit more than they'd expected, Maria hiked them back up right there in the middle of her speech and continued on with her analysis of Alan Greenspan's economic reasoning.

The speech must go on, and Maria knew that. She had a time limit to meet, sources to cite, points to make, judges to impress (at least with her speaking skills!), and competitors to knock out of the running. She wasn't about to let a little thing like public humiliation stand in her way! Recognizing that she had handled this skivvy situation with an undercurrent of humor, one judge even commented on the cute bulldog print! Choosing not to be mortified, choosing instead to calmly yet humorously deal with this uncomfortable situation, Maria demonstrated how, even though imperfection is unavoidable, looking it straight in the eyes is clearly admirable. Oh, and because you're probably curious, Maria placed second at that state tournament. Mischievous undergarments and all.

As a teacher, your job is not to remove the desire for perfection or the love of attention to detail—just to help the kids learn to manage it so that it doesn't get in their way. Help them remember that managing one's desire for success is usually coupled with inevitable obstacles.

We don't want to change who these kids are. Their dreams may require extreme attention to detail. Astronomers cannot afford to miscalculate by a tenth of a second or even a tenth of a degree. Perfectionism can become an important tool in the hands of a man or a woman who could save thousands, or millions, of lives someday.

Harriet Tubman said, "Every dream begins with a great dreamer. Always remember, you have within you the strength, the patience, and the passion to reach for the stars to change the world."

The perfectionism tool is invaluable; students just need to learn how to control it and use it wisely. And lucky you, that's where you come in!

6: Sense of Humor

> *"Humor is a spontaneous,*
> *wonderful bit of an outburst that just comes.*
> *It's unbridled, it's unplanned, it's full of surprises."*
> ~ Erma Bombeck ~

One of the most enjoyable characteristics of gifted individuals is a well-developed sense of humor. They delight in puns, in irony, and in the ability to see things in a different way. Their advanced intelligence allows them to pick up on the subtleties that others miss—the subtleties which distinguish between the ordinary and the hilarious. It is true that gifted children typically have more advanced senses of humor. They appreciate adult jokes (intellectual humor) because they know enough to understand what makes them funny. And when creating their own humorous moments, gifted students can take the mundane, add a little wit, and stir the mix until it tickles their ribs. Their brains have a natural way of looking at things from unusual angles—divergent thinking, or thinking "out of the box." Divergent thinking is often a pathway to humor, and individuals who are gifted with a great sense of humor adeptly utilize these tools to amuse, entertain, and enlighten those around them.

Erma Bombeck, popular syndicated humor columnist and author, took the most ordinary, everyday routines of her life and turned them into entertainment. She knew how to transform a simple task such as the changing of a toilet paper roll into an event worth laughing about.

The title of one of Bombeck's books declared *If Life Is a Bowl of Cherries, What Am I Doing in the Pits?* Her life was sometimes tragic. Her father died when she was young, she experienced childhood poverty, and she suffered from a disease that eventually ended her life. But through it all, she had a knack for seeing the lighter side. Even in the midst of "the pits," her brain couldn't help but see beyond the ordinary and find the extraordinarily humorous.

Gifted children are always on the lookout for the ironies in life. If knowledge is brain food, then humor is the dessert. And as Mary Poppins said, "A spoonful of sugar helps the medicine go down." Whether "the medicine" is personal hardships or an academic subject that may not otherwise catch their interest, a spoonful of humor makes it easier to swallow.

A sense of humor is a gift in itself. It is having a sense of gratitude for things that are different and unexpected. It holds originality and uniqueness in high esteem. It looks beyond the moment and into the bigger scheme of life.

Humor shows up when students look at something in new or unusual ways, as Tamara sees frequently. At the end of each school year, her students have an evening where they display and present their Advanced Studies projects and invite the whole community to come and see what they have studied and learned. One year, a couple of the parents pitched in to buy Tamara a dozen roses—bright red-orange roses—to thank her for all she had done for her students that year. The next day, Tamara was having a class discussion with seventh graders who had just completed the class and shown their projects for the first time. Seated in a circle, the students were offering their reflections on the process they had just come through. Tamara put the vase of roses on the floor in the middle of the circle to add some ambiance to the room. Within a few minutes, she noticed that some of the students had gradually (perhaps instinctively?) scooted closer to the roses and were rubbing their hands over the flowers as if warming them over the flames of a campfire! Campfires are a fairly common experience for Montana kids, and they usually involve the roasting of marshmallows, too. Sure enough, moments later, Ronny reached behind himself and grabbed a tissue, wadded it up, stuck it on the end of his pencil, and was holding it over the roses as if roasting a marshmallow over the campfire! The discussion with the students, meanwhile, continued at its normal pace, but underneath it, a second, nonverbal conversation was also taking place. Michelle and Leigh gestured to Ronny to hand them each a tissue, too, and soon the other students were roasting marshmallows as well. Except for Nadia. She had recently moved to Montana from a much warmer state, and the poor girl was a bit confused about what the others were up to!

A play on words is another favorite strategy among gifted children who utilize humor. Tamara sent a couple of students out to her car one day to carry in armloads of items for projects. She said, "While you're at it, please bring in *Stormy Seas*® [a puzzle game] from the trunk of my car." Momentarily looking confused, Vijay soon grinned and asked her, "So we're supposed to look for some cloudy letters while we're out there, too?" Cloudy letters? Stormy C's!

More word play: while eating a pickle at lunch one day, young Madelyne stood the remainder of it on its end and proclaimed it to be a balanced diet. Great! How did she come up with that one?

This sort of intellectual and sometimes zany humor fits wonderfully into those learning environments we call classrooms. The brightest students in Dr. Nickel's high school chemistry class loved to swap chemistry-related jokes with him:

What is the undertaker's favorite element? Barium!

What is a doctor's main profession? Helium!

What does the worst teacher you've ever had do? Boron!

What happened when the boy swallowed a bee? Tungsten!

Even the youngest gifted child can create some surprising jokes using words. Three-year-old Abel had learned not only the English alphabet, but also large parts of the Greek and Hebrew alphabets, plus many words in Japanese and Chinese. He put this knowledge to new use one night when getting out of the bathtub: he asked his mother to hand him his "tao."[9]

Abel's father worked at a university physics laboratory with a coworker who decided that little Abel needed to learn some less serious words, too, so he taught him some less formal, "hillbilly" vocabulary words like "purt-near" and "hootenanny" and "nary." At the pizza parlor one night, Abel pointed to an olive and called it an "olivet" (many letters from the Hebrew alphabet end in "-et"). When his father asked if that could have been a letter from one of the lost tribes of Israel, Abel replied, "Purt-near!"

Combining their knowledge with humor brings great joy to gifted children. One of the things they love about being around other gifted kids is being able to share their intelligent humor with others who actually "get it." They also love concocting their own funny ways of exploring what they know.

Oliver loved to play pranks, not to be malicious, but just because he thought they would be funny. One prank happened in science lab in middle school. He and his also-smart buddies were sitting at a lab station when they decided they wanted to see what would happen if they put a thin strip of magnesium into a breakered power outlet and then turned the power on. They all knew ahead of time what they *thought* would happen— it would explode in a massive flash of light, and it would create quite a stir. But they did it anyway. As light filled the room, the teacher raced back and asked what they had done. They explained exactly what they had done and how they had done it. And why did they do it? Because they wanted to confirm that what they expected to occur would, in fact, happen. Of course, they were rushed right off to the principal's office. They knew that they were going to get in trouble long before they flipped the switch, but it was such a ludicrous thing to actually do, they just *had* to do it, despite the consequences.

Smart kids are sometimes willing to do crazy and possibly dangerous things just to see what will happen, and they think it's funny. It usually *is* funny, at least from their perspective. But even when they *know* it will get them in trouble, they are still compelled to do it—because who else would think to do something so totally crazy? "That is an outrageous and possibly dangerous idea; we *have* to do it!" It is not unusual for some gifted children to believe that these types of pranks are genuinely funny. And when the grownups around them express shock or horror over their escapades, the kids are truly confused as to the reaction. Don't the adults get it? Under these circumstances, rather than an adult reacting with an immediate negative response, it might be best to sit down with the kids when the crisis is over and say, "You know, I understand why you would want to try new things, but do you realize what the consequences could have been?" They don't always think that far ahead and may need a little guidance in that area.

A group of Tamara's college friends in the honors dorm cooked up a silly experiment one night that involved two nails, a pickle, a cord from an old lamp, and a bit of electricity. All went well until they decided to leave it put together longer and ended up blowing all of the circuits in the building. It was a dark weekend until Monday rolled around and someone with the right key was able to open the locked circuit-breaker panel and switch their power back on!

Humor allows us to laugh, even when a particular situation would otherwise make us cringe or even become angry.

A few years ago, Tamara's seventh-grade gifted students were working on an assignment where they had to create a diagram or other visual depiction of the abstract ideas they had been discussing. One of the girls was using bottle paints for her visual depiction. These paints have a little sponge on the end through which the kids can dab, smear, or spot the color onto a paper surface. This girl apparently thought the red wasn't coming out red enough, so she shook it up vigorously to mix the pigments back in.

Despite the fact that the bottles and their lids had always been sturdy and secure, this bottle lost its top. The screwed-on lid and the sponge topper both came flying off mid-shake, followed by a long stream of dark red paint that spattered on the student's pants and left a gigantic seven-foot long swath of dark red liquid on the pale gray carpet in the classroom.

Uh-oh….

Anyone who works with children, whatever their ages and abilities, knows to expect the unexpected both in terms of the accident with the top coming off and in the kids' reaction to it. Children sometimes have an amazing knack for saying or doing things that we as adults would never think of. In that moment of shocked reaction when this girl stood gasping at the red paint on her new jeans and the rest of the class was frozen with their jaws hanging open, another student, Yurik, without so much as even a hint of a pause, threw himself onto the floor next to the giant red splotch, legs askew, elbow crooked at an odd angle, tongue hanging out of his mouth—the perfect pantomime mockery of a dead body. "Quick!" he shouted with genuine urgency. "Someone get a piece of chalk!" Because, of course, we should outline the body in the crime scene! Yurik suddenly saw another way to look at the situation and bring some humor to it and, in doing so, made everyone laugh. It's just like Erma Bombeck said, "If you can't make it better, you can laugh at it." Yurik took the edge off the potentially stressful situation involving red paint on clothes and carpet. Of course, it helps when the teacher can laugh and have fun right along with the kids and avoid the creativity killers—blocks to creativity—of being rigid and judgmental.

It helps if the teacher is willing to roll with things and have a little fun now and then, too. That same year, just for fun, Tamara played a little trick on her students. One day after school, she'd been sitting at her desk working quietly when the lights suddenly went off. But the computer was still on, so she knew it wasn't a power outage. When she stood up to go find out what was going on, the lights came back on. "Oh, wow," she thought, "I have motion-sensor lights in my classroom!" And she decided she could have a little fun with this interesting discovery.

Since she noticed the lights overhead buzzed slightly before they turned off, she cooked up a plan involving a very still classroom. The next day, she had the students work alone on a quiet assignment. She had also pushed the tables closer to the walls so the motion sensor on the ceiling in the middle of the room would be less likely to pick up small movements.

Before they began working, Tamara asked if anyone knew what telekinesis was.

"Isn't that where someone moves something with their mind?" Yurik asked.

"Yes, it is, and did you know that I have telekinetic powers?"

"No way! That stuff's not real!"

"Hmm. Well, maybe someday I will prove to you that I do. Now get to work!"

While the students began working, Tamara sat at her desk and listened carefully and patiently for the slight buzz of the lights.

About 15 minutes later, it happened.

"Watch this, everyone!"

She put her fingers to her temples and closed her eyes in concentration, humming to cover up the buzzing.

A second later the lights turned off and the students gasped in amazement!

"How'd you *do* that?!?"

"Teach me, teach me!"

Tamara eventually told them her secret.

Humor is one of the gifted teacher's greatest tools. It binds relationships and creates friendships and curiosity. Most students appreciate and can relate to a strong sense of humor in their teachers.

When Mrs. Brown, who was close to retirement, announced that she was working out in the weight room at noon with Mr.

Binther and Mr. Carlson, her students laughed at her and said, "Uh huh. Sure." So when she walked into her class one day in the middle of an arm-wrestling match between two students, she said, "Oh, I could beat you guys."

Well, the class decided to give her a break, a sort of handicap advantage. They told Karen's son Stanley, who isn't exactly Arnold Schwarzenegger, to arm-wrestle Mrs. Brown. He and she were both up for the challenge. "All right!" "Okay!"

The class gathered around as the two of them sat down and faced off. "Go! Go! Go!" the class chanted. Keep in mind here that Mrs. Brown is a drama teacher; her face was screwed up tight and her eyebrows met each other beneath the fringe of her snowy white hair. Stanley, whose eyebrows normally meet in the middle, clenched his jaw and twisted his mouth to the side of his face. They struggled. Their arms trembled.

Mrs. Brown won.

She won the match, the relationships, and the respect of her students—not for winning, but for playing.

Playing is part of the relationship.

The kids love Mr. Binther's high school science classes; in a small high school, he teaches chemistry, calculus, and physics. The kids never know what to expect from the guy. "What's he going to do today?" The suspense keeps them coming back for more.

Mr. Binther is the guy who drags his hockey puck or door-stop on a string as he walks down the hall, and if anyone looks at him funny, he says, "I'm walking Dot." Always expect the unexpected with Mr. B.

He's also been known to interrupt the morning announcements, which are televised and produced by students. One morning, while the two announcer persons were announcing, Mr. B. jumped in behind them and leaped around in an overcoat with a banana in hand. His motive for this has yet to be discovered.

Other times, he'll get right in front of the camera and say strange things. He might be wearing his school sweatshirt that day and start cheering for the football team. Or he'll run in out of the blue yelling, "Woohooooo!" and then run out again.

As one teacher said, "Some teachers are certified. Others are certifiable."

What is written all over Mr. Binther's face is enthusiasm and humor. It leaks out of everything he does. He uses humor as an outlet, a stress-reliever, a friend-maker, and an attention-getter. At the end of the year, when Stanley was studying Edgar Allen Poe in Mrs. Brown's English class, Mr. B. was invited in to talk about physics to help explain one of Poe's stories. Physics is not something Stanley finds particularly interesting. But after sitting at a desk and listening to Mr. B. for a half an hour, Stanley came home with a new appreciation for the mysteries of physics. He said he learned more in that half hour than he learned in an entire year in science class.

Karen asked him why? What makes Mr. B. such a good teacher?

Stanley replied, "He's funny, and he just keeps things going and makes everything interesting. He makes you think fast, and he calls on you and keeps you thinking. Gosh, maybe I'll take physics next year."

One of the pathways to a student's brain is through his funny bone. Humor relaxes the brain and gives lessons sticking power. Have fun with it. Laughing is supposed to be good for physical and mental health, so use it in the classroom whenever you can. Granted, some subjects—for example, the Holocaust—deserve a more solemn and respectful treatment, but you can still have fun with at least some of the history of World War II. And sometimes, when you bring humor in, you bring in a contrast. If everything is as serious as the Holocaust, the emotional and intellectual impact of that experience is lessened due to the monotony of mood. Take seriously what requires seriousness. Respect it. But sit back and laugh at some of the other stuff. Find the irony, have fun with all of that other interesting information you get to share with the students. Make them *want* to learn because it is so enjoyable and/or amazing.

Turn those chapter questions into *Family Feud* or *Hollywood Squares* or even *Survivor*. Give the winner a round trip pass to the restroom, all expenses paid, toilet paper provided. Make up funny words to a tune to help kids remember the facts. Let kids use humor in their projects and in their homework as long as they get the information straight. Be off the wall and out of the box.

We know a teacher who introduces his fifth-grade students to fractions by taking a pair of scissors and cutting his tie in half. He gets their attention every time. They look at him in shock, which makes sense. Their parents would kill them if they did something like that to their own clothing. Good move. Now, the next trick is to really suck them into the subject of fractions and percents and keep them there.

Humor is also a way to add a positive edge to a consequence for breaking the rules. When one high school teacher we know has to deal with tired students who fall asleep at their desk, he gives them a "negative" consequence—he throws a Nerf® ball at their shoulders and wakes them up. But hey, while accomplishing its purpose, the Nerf® ball (not to be confused with nerd ball) also provides some humor. The class laughs. The mood is lightened, not darkened. The kid wakes up and pays attention. Everyone goes on with the lesson. Mission accomplished.

Of course, this wouldn't fit with every teacher's style, but you can find something that works for you.

Humor may not be a cure-all, but it sure comes in handy in a thousand-and-one situations. Take stress, for example. Even though we've discussed the importance of having a sense of humor in situations involving stress, we can't emphasize it enough.

Ilene and Nan were pros at turning a stressful situation into a hilarious event. In high school, they were selected to participate in a statewide chemistry competition. This involved driving to a town about an hour away to take a test, and their parents let them make the trip on their own. Having never driven there by themselves before, they got confused when it came time to drive home and took a wrong turn, heading south on the interstate instead of north. Happily involved in comparing the answers they had given on the test, it was almost an hour later, when they reached the next sizable town, before they realized they'd gone the wrong way. With no quarter for the pay phone and no cell phone, they turned around 180 degrees, headed due north, and discussed how to ease their parents' worries and fears when they finally made it home. Well, a two-hour drive is more than enough time for a couple of bright, zany girls to write, compose, and practice a song whose lyrics playfully retell the day's adventure!

Stress is unavoidable but manageable. Humor is the biggest stress deflator we know. It takes all of the hot air out of a problem and reduces it to nothing but the wimpy, floppy, rubbery skin that it is. The problem is still real; it is still there, but you can see around it again. Humor puts things into perspective.

Bring humor into the classroom every chance you get. Welcome it. Classrooms can sometimes be very stressful places.

Some kids get test anxiety. Their brains freeze up, and the temperature continues to drop in proportion to the importance of the test. They can know the material inside and out, but put them under pressure, and every iota of information gets sucked into some yet-to-be-discovered black hole, only to be spewed forth again when their breathing and pulse rate have returned to normal.

Pop the balloon. Let the air out. Distract them with some lighter fare.

Mr. Binther likes to joke around with his students right before a test. One of his favorite things to tell his class is, "Well, I'm going down to the office to look at my Britney Spears website on the computer! You guys take your tests." That was before one of the students had to use Mr. B's computer for a project and came back to the classroom, saying, "Mr. Binther, you really *do* have Britney Spears on your computer!"

Mr. Binther was busted—and shocked. "What?" he said. "Well, I never saw it!"

"Suuuuure," the kids said. "Every day you say you go look at it, but now you say it's not on there." Later, the students discovered that his student teacher had put the website on his computer. Sounds like she was a gifted-teacher-in-the-making!

Sure, there are other things you can do to loosen up the kids before a test, but they don't always work. You can use relaxation techniques, but sometimes all that does is give a kid enough thinking space to focus on her worries. You can play games, sort of like warm-ups, but the test may still loom in front of the student's mental eyeballs where she can't see around it. Humor is a distraction that can stop the loop of anxiety, anger, or fear that sometimes plays over and over again in our brains. And for some kids, you could say, "I want you to imagine yourselves getting every problem correct." This will constitute humor for some but will change the mood to positive rather than negative.

Sometimes a well-planned practical joke is the "piece de resistance" for gifted kids. On her last day of high school before graduation, Catherine, the girl who wore all of the costumes earlier in our book, pulled a brilliant practical joke on her favorite teacher, Mr. Reuben, who taught physics. Sneaking into school extra early that morning, she spent a full hour setting up an elaborate array of booby-trapped water balloons, each correctly labeled, that incorporated each law of gravity and many of the other laws of physics. When you touched them, they spilled their water.

Tamara and her friend April eventually won a practical joke war in college by coming up with an idea for a joke that is still being played out to this day. The victim's room was toilet papered—only this pervasive fact was not immediately apparent. Every last piece of evidence was thoughtfully well-hidden. Socks were removed from the sock drawer, unrolled, toilet paper stuffed in them, rolled back up, and placed back in the sock drawer. Random envelopes in the envelope box were selected to receive a single square of toilet paper. Random pages in textbooks and notebooks were marked with single squares as well. The sleeping bag was unrolled, toilet paper stuffed into the bottom of it, rolled back up, and shoved back under the bed. The tennis racket cover was removed, a smiley face was woven into it with toilet paper, and the cover put back on. CD cases, clarinet pieces, pockets in winter coats, rolled up posters, and rarely-worn dress shoes became additional sites for hidden toilet paper. Years later, they occasionally get a phone call from that old friend saying, "Guess what I found today?!"

Tamara's students have been known to use similar tactics on her. Let's just say Tamara's desk is a little bit cluttered. Well, okay, it's an all-out mess. Isn't it true that a cluttered desk is a sign of genius? But she does clean her desk up from time to time, like prior to parent-teacher conferences, and when she does, she'll often find a note from a student, buried near the bottom, saying, "When you find this note, I'll buy you a soda." The student signs and dates it, too, no less!

This is the deal, the thing that makes humor so effective—it catches people off guard. Think about it: if you know the punch line to a joke, it isn't funny anymore because you know what to expect. Humor is the unexpected. It is spontaneous and unpredictable. And right when the brain determines to maintain focus, something unexpected blares across the radar screen and throws it off track. Even if it only works for a few minutes and brings a brief smile or turning up at the corners of the mouth, it's enough to give the brain a chance to regroup and relax so it can think clearly rather than intensely.

We heard about one teacher who hid in his classroom closet wearing a gorilla suit while his students sat at their desks, wondering where he was and whether they should tell the office that he was late, and also worrying about how difficult the test might be when he passed it out. Imagine their shock and surprise when he jumped out and roared. And it delighted them at the same time. Imagine what a relief it was to their brains that they had a chance to be distracted, even if it was only for a few seconds.

Humor has the power to beat stress, create friendships, and strengthen bonds. It helps us relate to one another. It allows us to relax and accept—even appreciate—our foibles and mistakes

Erma Bombeck said, "When humor goes, there goes civilization."

Growth in society often comes about when we can laugh at ourselves as we recognize our weaknesses. Once we recognize our weaknesses, we can strengthen and improve them.

In a classroom setting, laughter is a much more effective way than yawning to get oxygen to all of the brains. Appeal to all of their senses and all of the intelligences when you are teaching, but heavens to Betsy, don't forget that sense of humor.

7: Creativity and Divergent Thinking

"I cannot rest; I must draw, however poor the result."
~ Beatrix Potter ~

Without thinking too hard, see if you can fairly quickly name 10 creative people!

We'll let you ponder…. It's okay, take your time. Jot them down in the margin if you'd like.

Looking at your list, how many of the people whose names you listed are artists? Musicians? Writers? Probably most of them, huh?

Can a scientist be creative? What about a mathematician?

Are there any children on your list? Friends?

The ability to bring new ideas to life, to see something old from a unique perspective, or to solve a problem in ways most other people wouldn't think of is creativity. Creativity is the exploration and production of new and unusual ideas. Our world thrives on creativity. It keeps things moving along. We need new technology, new foods, better buildings, new ways to produce energy. Necessity may be the mother of invention, but creativity draws up the plans.

Many creative people are *driven* to create. Creating is as vital to life for them as breathing. Writers, artists, musicians all report a certain drive to do their work. And as Beatrix Potter indicated in the quote above, the outcome isn't necessarily the important thing. The important thing is often "simply" the process—the act of creating.

Have you ever tried to pull a creative student away from a project she is immersed in? Does she even notice that you're there trying to get her attention? Nope. Which very likely means she is in a state of "flow." Flow is a term coined by psychology professor Mihaly Csikszentmihalyi (don't worry, we can't pronounce his name either) to describe that state when a person is so thoroughly immersed in a creative act that she has reached peak production, doesn't notice the passage of time, and is almost in another world. Creative people are imaginational escape artists!

If you know a creative person (or are one yourself), you know how fulfilled and satisfying that creative person's life can be. The man with the long name above has described creativity as "a central source of meaning in our lives...[and] when we are involved in it, we feel that we are living more fully than during the rest of life."[10]

What is the state of creativity in our schools today? Is creativity only "handled" or "discussed" in the music or art classrooms? Are young budding scientists encouraged to explore new theories and experiment with new materials? Are our young mathematicians encouraged to find new creative solutions to math problems? How many of our students would envy Beatrix Potter when she said, "Thank goodness I was never sent to school; it would have rubbed off some of the originality."

Scary thought.

The bright side is, while some of you probably answered no to some of the questions above about creativity in our schools, some of you also answered yes. What a treasure to be a teacher, to be daily witness to the creativity and optimism of our collective future, to watch the evolution of minds happen right before your very eyes. It reminds us of teacher-astronaut Christa McAuliffe when she said, "I touch the future. I teach."

Sometimes, children use their creative problem-solving skills to overcome their lack of opportunities to be creative. Beatrix Potter was one. You remember, she wrote the popular children's stories about small animals with charming names like Peter Rabbit, Benjamin Bunny, and Squirrel Nutkin—and then illustrated her stories with her own painstakingly detailed paintings. Well, Beatrix grew up in Victorian times, the child of a wealthy Victorian family. Though her little brother Bertram was sent to school to learn, she never was because her parents didn't believe that girls needed an education. (We're glad things have changed in that regard.)

Thanks to a large inheritance, Beatrix's parents lived lavishly, while the children spent their days with governess after governess. Aside from summer trips to the countryside, young Beatrix and Bertram saw their parents only on rare occasions and holidays. Though tragic for her relationship with her parents, these circumstances actually allowed Beatrix to be creative, because her parents were not the sort to knowingly grant permission to some of the means by which she pursued her creativity.

Beatrix's love of drawing and her love of animals and science became intertwined early on. She would smuggle animals into the house so that she could observe them longer and more closely in order to be better able to draw them. She and her brother even skinned and dissected the dead animals they found outside so they could better understand their anatomy and draw them more accurately. It was through drawing, writing, painting, memorizing Shakespeare, and minutely observing the details of the natural world around her that Beatrix brought life and excitement to her otherwise lonely childhood. For children like Beatrix, creative pursuits are a means of survival. She had an inner drive to create. We know writers who simply have to write. Artists who have to draw. Musicians who have to play.

We don't want to take children's creativity away from them—for their sakes, and for ours. Not only does a creative mind promise unexpected solutions to problems now and in the future, but it also makes life more interesting for the rest of us as well. Children often have a need to spill out all of the cool stuff that's happening in their head. They've got information zipping around and ricocheting off the cells of their cute little gray matter, and it's looking for a little attention and appreciation and acknowledgement of its value. So it shoots out of their mouths to say, "Hey! Look at me! Cool huh? I've got more where that came from!" Creativity amuses us when, out of the mouths of babes, we hear a fantastic story or an innocent pun or a child's-sized view of the world. A kindergarten class is a good place to find some creativity.

In Mrs. Norton's kindergarten class, amid all of the soap-opera-plot show-and-tells, Kenny Watson took his turn. He had a watch to show, only there was nothing on his wrist.

Mrs. Norton asked, "Where is it?"

"It's right here. It's invisible."

"Oh? What does it do?"

"It can make me invisible."

Mrs. Norton's classroom aide, Mrs. Plume, a very kind but very mischievous woman, asked, "Can you do it right now?"

Kenny smirked, as though that were a silly question. "Not right now. I don't want to."

"What does it look like?" Mrs. Plume asked.

"It has lots of buttons to push, and they do different things."

"If you can't see the buttons," Mrs. Plume asked, how do you know what button to push?"

"Oh, I can tell," said Kenny.

Did Kenny know that his watch wasn't real? Of course. But the idea that it could be real, or at least should be real, was good enough for him.

Gregory is another student whose imagination is very real to him. He's still young enough that he hasn't quite begun to outgrow it yet. Although he's certainly smart enough to know the difference between reality and fantasy, the line gets blurred sometimes in his overactive imagination. One day, he proceeded to tell the rest of the second graders what he had eaten for dinner the night before. With great sincerity, he relayed details of fried slugs, candied ladybugs, creepy crawlies, grasshoppers, and roly-polys that had graced his family's dinner table. He happily answered questions about which were his favorites ("the fried slugs, of course") and which ones were the hardest to catch ("the creepy crawlies, because my mom wouldn't go after them herself"). Though his family didn't *really* eat bugs for dinner, in Gregory's highly creative young mind, the feast was as real to him as though it had happened. He could see it, smell it, and taste it. Creative ability adds richness to life.

It also causes us to smile inside at the same time that we're listening to this child's explanation. We don't want to spoil the child's fun by saying, "Oh, that's just pretend. It's not real." The child is already aware that his imaginary feast is not real. However, his brain is having fun with it, running free rather than running laps, getting exercise and fresh air. Enjoy the game with him. If other children in the class insist that his feast was impossible, then invite them to play the game, too. Say to them, "But imagine if it *were* real. What would that be like? How would it taste? How would you cook those bugs? Which would be *your* favorite?"

After all, everybody's brain needs a little fun time now and then. Besides, imagine where J.K. Rowling's[11] books would be if she didn't allow *her* brain a little fresh air and freedom from convention.

Mrs. Wallace likes to be creative along with her students. She teaches the gifted students in a school district that is on the same Indian Reservation where Tamara teaches. One day, she came to school dressed as the mother pig from the "Three Little Pigs" story. She was enjoying "Dress Up as Your Favorite Storybook Character Day" with her students. One of her students, Na'pic'ka, had come to school dressed as a witch from her favorite fairy tale. "Na'pic'ka" means "spirit" in the Kootenai tribal language, and this child certainly had an imaginative spirit.

"Mrs. Wallace, my parents are coming to school today." Her parents were very involved in the school, so this wasn't unusual.

"Okay. When will they be here?"

"Oh, they're *already* here," Na'pic'ka whispered as she raised the lid of a little bucket she had been carrying around.

Mrs. Wallace peeked inside to find two live frogs!

A good example of creativity. Creativity is the force behind the underground spring that often bubbles up to the surface as humor. It gives new perspective to the ordinary or the usual. It creates new adventures and turns boring, everyday subjects into unforgettable, brain-etching experiences. It can even happen in college.

A college freshman tells a story of a Montana professor who taught college chemistry by adding a little creativity to bring the lesson to life. He was explaining limiting reactants to his class through the example of ingredients for s'mores, a favorite dessert usually made around the campfire. He said, "I have four graham crackers, eight marshmallows, and six squares of chocolate. Which is the limiting reactant?" Then he asked his class of approximately 300 students if there was anyone who had not tasted a s'more before. (For those who may not know, it's a delicious snack made with chocolate squares and melted marshmallow squished between two graham crackers and usually eaten by a campfire out in the woods while camping or picnicking. It's called a s'more because it's good enough to want "some more.")

Since one Asian student raised his hand, the professor turned on a projector which displayed a picture of some desert (yes, that's *desert*, not *dessert*) plateaus on a two-story high screen. He then dimmed the lights, turned on a John Denver album to add further ambiance, and proceeded to light a bowl of alcohol on fire to roast a marshmallow. He then made a s'more and gave it to his Asian student to eat.

What happened here? Well, he interrupted his lecture with a multi-sensory experience that, on the surface, had little to do with the subject. In the process, however, one student not only experienced his first s'more, but every other student in the class experienced it with him vicariously, and undoubtedly, it was an experience they will always remember. That experience planted ideas in their heads—ideas that they will always associate with "limiting reactants."[12] (Oh, and if you haven't yet figured out the answer to the professor's question, you can find it in the endnotes.)

Now, let's take something as simple as subtraction and regrouping. Why in the world would a class of second graders care about regrouping? Can we add some creative problem-solving here? Mrs. Norton was subbing for a few days in second grade, and she tried to find an answer for that question. It was around Easter vacation time, and the kids in her class certainly cared about Easter candy and Easter eggs. How could she bring in some excitement?

Well, she brought in jellybeans and some plastic eggs, the kind that come apart and you can put something inside. She decided to make the jellybeans the "ones," and 10 "ones" were counted out and placed in each plastic egg to make the "tens." Then 10 plastic eggs were placed in a see-through net bag to make the "hundreds." In this way, she taught regrouping. She showed the children how to get to the number 25 by using two filled eggs and five jellybeans. Then she taught them regrouping by saying, "Now, take away jellybeans until you have 17."

They tried, but they couldn't do it with just the five beans, so they had to open one of the eggs. The rule was that if they opened an egg, they had to crack it open over their heads, which is not only fun but can be used as helpful imagery when teaching them to regroup later. As soon as they cracked an egg open, they knew to scratch off one of the eggs that they had on their paper. They could see that they had 15 beans in their hand and one egg left, and they went from there. The hands-on experience, both tangible and visible, played an important part in their understanding of the system. Maybe the sugar factor also played a part. Because every kid knows the value of keeping close track of his candy.

Using concrete (plastic egg and jellybean) examples that the students can relate to will help them understand concepts that they don't understand or that are new to them. So now use your own creativity to make concepts interesting and, from the students' point of view, worth the brain space. Heck, if you can find a lesson in a bunch of plastic eggs and some jellybeans, imagine what you can find in more complicated forms of life.

Beatrix Potter is known for the story of Mr. McGregor chasing Benjamin Bunny out of his garden, along with many other stories and illustrations that go with the series. She was also a good creative problem solver. It turns out that in addition to sketching and writing stories, Beatrix began keeping a daily journal when she was 15 years old. She wrote faithfully in it until she was 30. But it wasn't until nearly 20 years after her death that anyone read it. Was this because it was hidden away? Nope. It was because the gifted young Beatrix had created a code in which she wrote her journal entries, a code so complex that it took an engineer seven years to decipher it.

That was quite a feat for a young girl, to come up with a code so complicated it took years to figure it out. But she was concerned with protecting her privacy. That was the problem she wanted to solve. Imagine how much fun she had solving it—and how much more satisfying it would have been to her had she lived long enough to see the enormous challenge it presented to the one who finally decoded it!

But let's go back to the classroom and the whiteboard. The students are waiting.

One way to incorporate creative problem-solving in your classroom is to use some creative resources. Karen's grandma, Mrs. Chrisman, remembers one of her college professors saying that a good school takes advantage of a good custodian, because that custodian has so much knowledge to add. So Mrs. Chrisman took the advice; she often invited the custodians into her classroom to help explain things she couldn't, and the custodians were always happy to help out. It was another kind of problem solving.

Remember, being creative requires you to look at something or someone from a new and different perspective. Everyone thinks about inviting doctors and scientists in as speakers. That's peachy. Sure, they have a lot to offer, but don't limit yourself to the obvious. Look around. What other untapped resources are out there just waiting to be utilized? Get creative with your resources. Schools are expected to meet every need under the sun, but they've only been given a handful of recruits to do the job of a full battalion.

People are connected to your curriculum in ways you might not have thought about. The baker can talk about science and how yeast and other leavening agents react to make bread rise. Lilly Anne's grandma, the little old lady in the brown and green house down the street, can share what she knows about local history, and maybe even history from the generations before her from the Old Country. Invite a Native American in if you want to bring that history to life. Don't stop with the textbook or take it as the whole story for everything. Don't let the kids think their textbook is the be-all, end-all of knowledge.

Along those same lines, we can be open-minded about gifted thinkers in our classrooms who find an answer to a problem in a new and unique way. It happens regularly with gifted children.

In the field of gifted education, Rachel McAnallen is a well-known mathematics instructor and presenter. In fact, thousands in our world (adults and children alike) know her as "Ms. Math." She uses the following example in her teacher training workshops:

Back when she was still teaching high school math, a student came along whose divergent thinking and problem-solving ability created a life-altering lightbulb moment for Rachel. A Chinese proverb says, "When the student is ready, the teacher will come." In this case, the "student" was the teacher.

The problem on the board was something like this:

$$47$$
$$\underline{-\ 18}$$

This was a remedial math class for students who weren't doing well in regular math.

Charlie raised his hand, and she called on him to tell her what to do first.

"Subtract the 1 from the 4," he said.

Well, that was all wrong! We all know you can't subtract from the left! And she told him just that.

"Oh yes, you can," he replied.

"Oh no, you can't," she asserted back.

"Yes, you can."

She decided to let him try it because she just knew it wouldn't work. She figured he simply needed to see it for himself.

"Okay, so if I subtract the 1 from the 4, what do I get, Charlie?"

"Thirty."

She wrote down 30.

"What do I do next, Charlie?"

"Subtract the 8 from the 7, and you get −1. Write it after the 30."

She did so and gasped:

$$47$$
$$\underline{-\ 18}$$
$$30\text{-}1$$

The answer was 29, and Charlie had just solved the problem by doing something every teacher he had ever had had told him was wrong: subtracting from the left.

Charlie instinctively knew that the 4 wasn't really a 4; it was a hidden 40. And the 1 wasn't really a 1; it was a hidden 10. And 40 minus 10 *is* 30!

Maybe Charlie shouldn't have been in remedial math after all. Maybe he hadn't "made it" in the regular math classes because his divergent mathematical thinking wasn't "the right way" to solve the problems. Maybe Charlie really *had* understood math all along.

Maybe it was the teachers who hadn't understood Charlie.

Minister and children's television star Fred Rogers once said during an interview, "Children are very valuable—not for who they would (or will) be, but for who they are." And they *are* usually a lot more capable than we give them credit for—especially when a little divergent thinking comes into play. Like Charlie's new way to do subtraction.

Creativity and divergent thinking are connected at the hip. Creativity is the desire and the ability to produce new ideas, products, etc., and divergent thinking makes it all possible. However, divergent thinking is often not a conscious act—it is just how certain brains work, and it makes for some interesting situations and dilemmas.

Divergent thinkers are nonconformists who much prefer their own way over the supposedly tried-and-true way. They see many possibilities, where convergent thinkers only see one right answer. They can find more than one answer on the test, which sometimes puts the grading to the test. Divergent thinkers can be a frustrating bunch to deal with, partly because divergent thinkers are not always a good match for those convergent places that are often called schools.

The frustration can go both ways. As one frustrated girl said about another student, "She's so *convergent!*" As if being convergent were the worst thing that could be said about a person. With gifted kids, divergent thinking comes with the territory. Imagine what it's like to be an outlier in a world designed for the average bunch. Things are going to add up differently for you.

Divergent thinkers are often the inventors, the dreamers, and the problem solvers in our world. Their daydreaming sometimes results in wonderful solutions to problems.

Jules Verne[13] was a divergent thinker. Though he attempted to shape his life to fit the wishes and expectations of his time and of his father, he still couldn't get away from his widely differing desires and ideas. As the eldest son of a lawyer, it was his father's expectation that Jules would go to the city (in this case, Paris) and become a lawyer, too. And although his father was paying for this opportunity, the money was swiftly taken away when it was discovered that young Jules was spending more time on his writing than he was on learning the law. Well, this turned out to be a blessing in disguise. Jules now needed a way to make money on his own, for which he relied on his best talent, his gift with words. He wrote short stories, plays, and many works which hold the distinction of being the most translated of all writings in history. His best known titles are *Around the World in Eighty Days*, *20,000 Leagues Under the Sea*, and *Journey to the Center of the Earth*.

It was in his writings that Verne's divergent thinking was most apparent. Decades before they would exist in reality, Verne conceived such things as submarines, space travel, rockets, helicopters, television, movies with sound, moving sidewalks, and heavier-than-air flying craft. While it is true that somewhere in the world at the time, a few inventors were working on prototypes of some of these ideas, not all of that was known to Verne. His fictional submarine *Nautilus*, for example, was "powered" by electricity a full 11 years before the lightbulb was even invented. He wove such detail and knowledge-based information into these science fiction enterprises that readers everywhere began to wonder, "What if...."

Some of Verne's ideas later came to fruition without the world ever knowing they were his ideas. In 1863, he wrote a novel titled *Paris in the 20th Century* that described such wonders as gas-powered automobiles, glass skyscrapers, a world-wide communications network, electric calculators and computers, and super-high-speed trains. Sounds like the 20th Century, doesn't it? Verne's publisher refused to print the book at the time. So he locked it away in a safe where it was found by his great-grandson more than 100 years later in 1989. This novel was finally published in 1994, when many of the things he predicted had already become a reality.

Imagine having a thinker like that in your classroom! Maybe you do. And in the midst of everything else you have to do, that divergent thinker isn't always easy to deal with, is she?

Give your students permission to continue in their creative pursuits. Give them the courage to be different, to be fulfilled, to take creative risks. Show them how it's done. Creative people are *so* interesting—and often happiest when they're creating.

Okay, you're a teacher. You have a room to decorate, you have a curriculum to cover, you have classroom rules to enforce, you have parents to deal with. Are you going to handle all of this the same way as the teacher across the hall? Probably not. You're two different people. You want to be allowed to tackle problems your way, using your own style, your own talents. You don't want to be forced into a mold and be told, "From now on, all teachers will study Mrs. Perfecto and take notes on her every move. You will all duplicate her classroom, her lesson plans, her discipline, her grading system."

Nah! We can't see you going for the carbon copy thing. You have more self-respect than that. The kids in your classroom? They're the same way. And if you try to force them to be someone other than who they are, you could end up with a few personal mutinies—otherwise known as power struggles. And while some of those mutinies will be obnoxious and aggressive, and some will be quiet, passive, and undetected. The relationships you have with your students will suffer either way. So will their education.

These divergent kids are sometimes the most challenging. It takes a special person to reach into the deep recesses of an artistic five-year-old brain and find a way to explain to her that drawing her entire family nude and in detail is not a good decision for the class phone book, which will be distributed to each child in the class and sent home in their backpacks. We don't suppose it would win the Mother's Choice Award for prime hang-it-on-the-refrigerator material either. But it *is* a good example of divergent thinking. She did the assignment the way it made sense to her.

We already mentioned that kindergarten is a good place to find divergent-thinking kids. Those little school newbies have a fresh way of thinking about things. They have not yet been pressed into the mold and squeezed and trimmed and sanded down until they meet the standards. We hope their teachers recognize that freshness and originality are things to be handled with care.

What if we discovered that the desire for preteen and teen and even adult conformity starts not with peers, but with those very first teachers who imply that there are rules and there are standards and ideals, and they are the same for every child. "I am looking for only one right answer, the answer *I* determine to be correct." Does that set the mold for later conformity?

Correct answers are sometimes in the interpretation. During Dental Health Month, a question on a worksheet in Jay's second-grade classroom asked, "How many permanent teeth do you have?" While the other kids were poking their fingers around in their mouths or counting teeth with their tongues, Jay simply answered, "Zero." Yet his teacher knew he had some permanent teeth, and she knew he understood the concept of "permanent teeth." She was also perceptive enough to know that Jay was a divergent thinker, so she asked him why he wrote down "zero."

"Well, no tooth is ever actually permanent. They can still fall out, especially when you get really old."

Divergent thinking. Lightbulb moment!

If the question had asked, "How many *adult* teeth do you have?" he probably would have counted his teeth, but the word "permanent" gave the question a whole different twist for Jay. As written, the question was simply assessing "Can the child count?" and "Does the child know what permanent teeth are?" Well, obviously Jay had long known how to count, and it was clear by his explanation that he knew what "permanent" ("adult") teeth were, so his teacher let him go ahead and be divergent and answer "zero."

Being open to these kinds of moments with kids is not always easy. As adults, most of us have probably already had most of that creative and divergent spice squeezed out of us. Besides, there's comfort in our ways, and there's stability in "the way things have always been done." So when we're teaching something "the way it's always been done" and a student comes along who tries to "show us the light," it's only human to put up some resistance.

Recently, Karen was mentoring a third-grade student in the Extended Studies program at her school. The boy, Nigel, was working on a rocket project and needed to measure the length of his rocket's flight. The problem required multiplication with decimals, so Karen said, "You need to come up with an answer on your own, but I'll do the problem, too, so we can compare and make sure the answer is right." So Karen sat there working the figures in a traditional manner, oblivious to Nigel, who had finished a few seconds after he started. He'd figured out his own way to calculate the problem. It was an estimate, but it was only a few feet off, and it was much faster than Karen's method. You see, Nigel hadn't yet learned how to do the traditional, written-out multiplying of decimal points, so he was unhampered by other people's thinking. His own way was more efficient. Estimation is a valuable skill.

One day, Karen's three-year-old son Rupert held up two fingers and said, "Mommy, I have two eyes, and one nose."

Eager to help him improve his counting skills, she said, "No, you have two eyes," she held up two fingers, "and one nose," and she held up one finger.

"No, Mommy," he said, still holding up two fingers, "I have two eyes and one nose. See?" At which point he held the two fingers up to his eyes and placed his nose neatly in the space between. He had been counting the nose with the single space, not the two fingers. He came from a fresh angle that Karen had been too experienced and wise to comprehend without his explanation.

Sometimes the best way to grow a happy brain is to give the kids less time to "learn" (as in memorize, regurgitate, recite, which is all convergent thinking) and more opportunity to *think* and *dream* and *imagine* on their own.

Consider this little gem once said by General George S. Patton:[14] "If everyone is thinking alike, then somebody isn't thinking."

And don't let too many rules get in the way, either.

Rules are good and necessary, but they can be taken too far. Decide which rules are the most important, and learn to let the other stuff go. Take the little girl who showed up at school with a flower sticker on the tip of her nose—some teachers might have demanded the prompt removal of the distracting bit of paper, but thankfully, not *her* teacher. This little girl was allowed to wear it all day long, and perhaps had a better day because of it, as she went about her business secretly feeling that the little flower on her nose set her apart and made her special.

Children need to experiment and think on their own as they develop a sense of self. As they get older, they need to know that those things that make them different also make them special. After all, people are special only because each individual is a limited resource, irreplaceable, never to be copied, unlike any other.

Makumbu was five years old when he asked his mom, "If God is holding the whole world in His hands, how come His fingers don't cover up some of the states?"

His brain was obviously concerned with some of the less typical questions in life.

Gifted kids come up with some wonderful questions. They also sometimes think outside the box just to relish having fun and being different, or maybe to experiment with a new, even temporary self.

Richie, a seventh grader, came to class one day with a chunk of his hair gelled up and sticking straight up on the top of his head. Apparently he had seen one of the girls using some gel at her locker and was curious what it was. After a quick lesson from the girl, he slicked up his hair and became a human unicorn. When he arrived at class that day, his first request was to borrow a ruler so he could measure it and see how high it was! Despite the snickering from some of the other students, he went through the rest of the day like that.

It's no surprise that Catherine (our two-week passion girl from an earlier chapter) never passed up an opportunity to come to school dressed in a costume. Not only did she consistently participate in Spirit Week each year (you know, Toga Day, Cowboy Day, Pajama Day, etc.), but any other random occasion was cause enough for Catherine to deck herself in an assortment of unusual garb. Just as she had come to school dressed as Princess Leia, buns and all, on opening day of the latest *Star Wars*™ movie, she did the same when the first *Spiderman*™ movie came out. She came to school dressed in a shiny red plastic dress that she had made, complete with blue yarn stretched across the outside of it in the pattern of a spider web. She loved to try out different characters.

So much about gifted children is outside the box—their ideas, fashion tastes, abilities, use of language, energy level, and perceptions of the world around them. Without support from a gifted program and/or an understanding parent or teacher, they can grow up feeling like outcasts, wondering why they're so different and what's "wrong" with them.

Being a divergent thinker in a seemingly convergent world is not always easy. While some divergers will enjoy and revel in their differentness, others will struggle to both fit in and be themselves. Developing and appreciating one's own identity can be hard enough. Imagine the challenge to do so when everyone around you thinks you're "too smart for your own good" or weirder than Weird Al, not using your talents appropriately, or wasting your time on impossible dreams. Being an adult in the life of a young divergent thinker is equally challenging. How do we encourage uniqueness and yet also help them to thrive in a world that may not always appreciate their differentness? It can be a delicate balance.

Really, is it more important that these kids fit in with everyone else, though often miserable in doing so, or is it better they happily be themselves, though risking the scorn of some of the averages? French author and philosopher Voltaire knew this struggle: "Our wretched species is so made that those who walk on the well-trodden path always throw stones at those who are showing a new road." But where would we be without those looking for a new road? Maybe stuck in a muddy rut.

Gifted teachers often have an instinctive ability to make every kid feel special because they recognize it as truth. They tolerate, accept, appreciate, and encourage their students' divergent thinking. They love the beautifully unexpected ideas. They are often divergent thinkers themselves. They think out of the box. They like to teach out of the box.

Your mission: Get 24 students to become one with the year's assigned curriculum. Mission impossible? Ha! Mrs. Norton, a fourth-grade teacher, says that the gift of teaching is being inspired as little ideas pop into your head to help you meet the needs of the kids. That's the fun part.

There is more than one way to handle any given problem. Develop your divergent-thinking skills. Find the best solution. The kids deserve the best.

When Karen's mom, Mrs. McGillicuddy, worked in the reading lab at school, she was faced with a dilemma. She had three young Mexican boys who needed to learn how to read but didn't speak any English. Their teacher didn't speak any Spanish. Mrs. McGillicuddy didn't speak any Spanish—at least not beyond saying "Hola" for "Hi" and "Baños?" for "Where is the bathroom?"

Hopeless? Naw. It was just a matter of getting creative. Mrs. McGillicuddy went through each beginning reader with them in three steps. First, she read it to them in English. Then she helped them read it to her in English. Then she had them explain it to her in Spanish while she repeated what they said to her. The boys certainly thought her pronunciation was worth chuckling over.

This was a give-and-take situation in which Mrs. McGillicuddy acknowledged the dignity and abilities of her students. During their retelling of the story in Spanish, they demonstrated their comprehension of the events in the book, and it gave them an opportunity to teach her and feel as though they had something to offer her, which they did. People learn more by teaching than from being on the other end, perhaps because it often requires more active brain involvement as they search for a way to communicate ideas.

Keep in mind that these were beginning readers reading simple books. The plot was easy enough to communicate even in a foreign language. There were other solutions to the problem, and different people might have taught English in a different manner.

Textbooks are dandy—they may even come in handy every now and then—but textbooks are like pieces of dry bread. We like the motto, "Students shall not live by textbooks alone." So dress them up and use them to make a Dagwood sandwich with a layered variety of activities and ideas. Skip the conventional and go for the interesting. Take the path less traveled rather than the path of least resistance. Pretend that you are the first person to develop a way to present those ideas and knowledge. You can have the same goal, but you don't necessarily have to have the same method. How would you go about getting the information across? Can you take your ideas and make them even better?

Karen remembers when she began learning about plants in school. Each student was given a bean seed to grow. First, they let it soak, and they placed it between a Mason jar and a wall made of moist paper towels, and in a few days, they watched the miracle of life as the seeds began to sprout. Fascinating! This lesson is also used in about every classroom under the sun. It's a good idea, but why stop there when there's so much potential left in that bean and in those brains? The experiment is over before it really even begins. The following story will illustrate a rather unique way to use plants in a lesson.

Mrs. McGillicuddy offered to help one teacher with her third-grade class when their science unit covered plants, but she took the extra-terrestrial perspective. The first thing she did was to sucker the class in with an art project using plastic one-gallon milk jugs. She had the kids cut them into helmets and decorate them with tubes and wires and other space alien-appropriate items. As they worked, their enthusiasm and anticipation for the adventures they would have as space explorers grew. Then she told the kids to put on their helmets, because they were her crew. She and their teacher would be the commanders. They were on a journey to an unfamiliar solar system—ours—and their job was to explore the planets to see which ones would support life. The experiment they would use involved growing plants, so that was the first thing they were going to study.

Every day at science time, the children donned their milk-jug helmets before they began their lesson. They learned all there was to know about growing tomato plants. They planted the seeds and nurtured them until they had healthy plants about five inches tall. They spent a lot of time on those leafy life forms, and most of the students became emotionally attached to them.

This made things a little more difficult when it came time to implement the rest of the experiment. Commander McGillicuddy stood in the front of the class and announced, "It is time to test out the planets. Gather your tomato plants, and you will receive your assignments." She divided the kids into three groups—Mercury and Venus, Earth and Mars, and then the outer planets. The kids knew what was coming, and with the exception of the Earth and Mars group, the class was in a pitifully emotional state, sniffling and tearing up.

The Mercury and Venus group held their plants closely and followed Mrs. McGillicuddy as they marched solemnly down the hall. Other teachers stood outside their classroom doors and watched, wondering at the sober looks. What had the kids done wrong, and why were they carrying tomato plants? The kids marched until they reached the room with the ovens. They then placed their plants in the barely warm ovens, bid their plants adieu, and returned to the classroom. As they returned, still sniffling, their teacher met them at the door and gave Mrs. McGillicuddy the evil eye as if to say, "You've made my children cry!"

It was then time for the Earth and Mars group to go. They marched off in big smiles, making feeble attempts not to gloat, and went into another classroom where they placed their beloved plants on a beautiful sunny window ledge.

After they returned, Commander McGillicuddy marched off another sober group—the outer planet group—to the teachers' refrigerator. They dutifully placed their plants inside and moped all the way back. Their teacher said, "Oh great, now that you've broken their hearts, you give them back to me to have for the rest of the day?"

Mrs. McGillicuddy smiled. "Well, at least they're going to get the point of why it's so important to have the atmosphere and all of the conditions we have on Earth. They're seeing it first hand."

The following day, it was time to see what the experiments had yielded. Mrs. McGillicuddy warned them ahead of time. "Now, we must remember that we're scientists. Being a scientist isn't always easy." The kids, other than the fortunate middle-planet few, marched in turn down the hallway, morose, dejected, a green, dead plant funeral procession. Mercury and Venus kids, even though they didn't expect their plants to survive, were devastated when they opened the oven and found that their plants had shriveled up to dried-up stubs. The Earth and Mars kids were thrilled to find their plants as lovely as when they had deposited them the day before. The outer-planets group were relieved to find their plants fairly normal looking when they opened the refrigerator door. Unfortunately, they watched over the next few days as their plants died a slow and agonizing death.

The students went back into the classroom and had a meaningful discussion on which of the planets could support life and which couldn't and why. This discussion was extraordinary because the students had become emotionally involved. And even though they were a little disconcerted by the experience, it was temporary. They talked about how they had to look at things as scientists, because they were alien scientists, and that was just part of what they were going to have to do to figure it all out.

Teaching tools are everywhere! Sure, you can dissect earthworms, but have you ever thought about dissecting a lightbulb? Or an old tennis shoe? How about a magic marker? Use it to show the kids about capillary action. Take it apart and let the kids see what's inside. They want to know what's inside.

Keep in mind that two of the most popular questions kids ask are, "Who says?" and "Why?" Those are good questions to ask. Encourage them to keep it up. If they really want an answer, they'll work for it. "The law says." Well, where in the world did that law come from? Whose big idea was it anyway? Why?

How can you give children information that stimulates their thought processes and has meaning and context, as well as longevity? Information can be given, but knowledge is earned.

The student has to work for it to understand and appreciate it and make it his own. The teacher's job, and the problem which requires all of the creative and divergent solutions, is to make the student *want* to work for it.

One teacher turned his entire classroom into a museum of history, while another third-grade teacher created a rainforest in her classroom. Gifted teachers have the ability to transform their classrooms into almost anything. Just like a good book, a gifted teacher, a divergent-thinking teacher, can take you anywhere in the world and beyond. They are time travelers. They are adventurers. They are not bound by gravity or atmosphere, by budgets or curriculum, by languages or cultures, or by traditional thinking patterns. They take wild hare-brained ideas and run with them. They aren't afraid to say to the kids, "I'm not sure if this will work. This will be an experiment for all of us. Let's see what happens!" They are always looking for a new and better way.

When Mrs. McGillicuddy worked with a class on World War II, she made ration books for each student. The students were expected to eat a limited amount of sugar during a given time, and they were to use their ration books to help them keep track.

She also made some small silhouettes of different types of aircraft from that period. She attached the silhouettes to the top of a flashlight, took all of the children in a dark room, and "flew" the plane shadows across the ceiling. The children were supposed to identify each plane and decide whether it was an enemy or friendly aircraft.

Another teacher asked his fifth graders to put their heads down on their desks, close their eyes (without falling asleep), and imagine the setting as he read a description of what life was like in the trenches of World War I. Suddenly, in the middle of the description and without warning, he made a loud booming sound to imitate a grenade. The kids jumped out of their seats. They got a little bigger taste of the trenches than they had expected they would when they laid their heads down and shut their eyes.

We know a high school history teacher who literally kicks the bucket (a metal wastebasket) whenever he gives a lecture about one or more historic figures who has "kicked the bucket." It gets the students' attention and also keeps the sleepy ones awake.

Lectures by themselves don't work. Something in each student has to be engaged in order for learning to take place. The teacher has to get them thinking, really listening, seeing, touching, feeling. Every sense should be used whenever possible, including their other senses, such as humor, logic, justice, and even their sense of reality. In order for them to want to learn, the subject should have meaning to them. They have to have some relationship with the information.

Gifted teachers use their own divergent thinking skills to find a way to speak to their students in a language they understand. A teacher is a unique and interesting individual presenting knowledge and thinking opportunities to a group of fresh individual brains who all have the capacity to process it in their own unique ways and turn it into who knows what and run in every direction with it.

A teacher has the opportunity to teach in a way that no other person can. What a deal!

8: Persistence

*"Nearly every man who develops an idea works it up to the point
where it looks impossible, and then he gets discouraged.
That's not the place to become discouraged."*
~ Thomas Edison ~

The ability to hang on through thick and thin has helped many an individual in life to overcome obstacles, achieve varying levels of greatness, and accomplish not only goals, but even perceived impossibilities. Ol' Thomas Edison[15] is a fine example of this. He ended up with more than 1,000 patents with his name on them. Who would have thought that all of those cool and wonderful things could have come out of one persistent man's brain? Of course, he also tried his hand at designing cement furniture, which, unlike the Wright brothers' invention, didn't exactly "take off." Probably because it was too heavy. And it was going to be painful to stub your toe on it in the middle of a dark, moonless night.

But no matter how bumpy the ride, Edison didn't give up, and he didn't let go of his ideas. So as annoying as it can sometimes be when gifted children are persistent, the gift of "hanging on" or persevering is not a gift to return for refund or exchange.

A first-grade teacher we know makes it a point to be flexible. She wants to encourage creativity and independence in children and allows them to make as many decisions as possible when it comes to their personal work. But there was one instance when she wanted a certain type of picture from each student, as she had plans to use those pictures on a bulletin board. One of the boys had a tough time, because he wanted to do it his way. She said, "Any other time, that would be fine, but this one time, I want you to do it my way."

He finally gave in. So while all of the other children drew their assigned 8x10 pictures, he drew his, too. Only he drew his the size of a postage stamp. He did what she wanted, but he still did it his way. He persisted in maintaining both his individuality and his creativity.

Unfortunately, persistence can be "educated" right out of a gifted child. Because if everything is easy for you year after year, will you know how to persist when something more difficult comes along?

In the children's book *The Story of Ferdinand*, by Munro Leaf, Ferdinand the bull chooses to take it easy every day, smelling flowers beneath the cork tree instead of wrangling with the other bulls. One day, he's stung by a bee and understandably reacts with a big to-do of anger and aggression toward the bee. Those witnessing his reaction assumed him to be the strongest of the bulls. Selected, as a result, to take on a matador in the bullring, he is woefully ill-prepared for the task. Rather than take on the challenge of the approaching matador waving the big flag, he opts to literally sit it out. Because he had eased through his days smelling flowers, he didn't know how to do that which he was capable of doing. As one reviewer of the book wrote, "He is praised all around for his power, until the day of his bullfight."

Our gifted children often experience the same thing! We praise them for their power, but not for what their efforts are in the bullfight. In some cases, they are able to slide through the system without ever experiencing a real challenge; then, on the day of their bullfight, which may be in high school for some or in college for others, when they first hit that first hard subject that requires serious study, they are ill-prepared, lacking the study skills and perseverance needed when it comes to facing challenges.

Persistence is psychological muscle. Just as a person's muscles will atrophy with lack of use, so can one's ability to be persistent. Gifted children in the primary grades often breeze through those years of school. They develop a false assumption that school (and everything else in life) will always be that easy. They come to believe that they should always be able to do something successfully the first or second time they try. Why should they believe anything else, when every academic experience they've had has only served to confirm this? Then, as they progress through advancing grade levels and the work becomes more difficult, they don't always know how to stick with a task to learn the material, because so far in school, they haven't had to use those persistence skills. During their elementary years, their teachers reinforced the idea that they were good students because they got good grades. Nobody told them that being a good student meant that they worked hard and overcame obstacles or challenges to get good grades. And certainly, no one ever told them that a hard-earned C was a more meaningful badge of honor than an easy A.

Tamara was part of an Honors College program at her university. Students were chosen for having high ability and potential and were scheduled into challenging classes with top professors. The sad thing was that a couple of those kids dropped out of college. They were supremely intelligent, yet they couldn't handle college, a place where they should have done well. Suddenly something was really difficult for them, and they had no skills or tools to deal with it because they had never had to work at learning before. How very sad to lose those bright minds.

Certainly all children, and all adults for that matter, can benefit in life from being persistent. Persistence is by no means unique to the gifted. But it has been observed as a trait quite common among those who achieve, discover, overcome, and create.

Like Edison, children are going to deal with both success and failure, and we need to find ways to prepare our gifted youth for dealing with both. There *will* be times they will have to face failure.

Two of Tamara's students once provided her with a great example of the benefits of built-up persistence skills. Ford and Lew were in her Advanced Studies class at the middle school. As seventh graders, it was the first time they had taken the class, and therefore it was the first time in their educations that they had to be so independent in their learning. As a teacher, Tamara sometimes feels like a mother whose child is learning to ride a bicycle. (You know there will be stumbles and skinned knees, but you also know you have to let them try.) She recognizes the importance of letting her students take their own steps in their learning. In the long run, this is the very best thing for them, because there won't always be a teacher to tell them what to learn and how to learn it. We want our students to be lifelong learners, yet we seldom allow them to learn how to learn on their own—the very thing they need if they are to be lifelong learners.

For their project, Ford and Lew wanted to learn about aerodynamics and the mechanical workings of an RC (remote-controlled) airplane. They wanted to take an RC plane apart and dissect its inner workings, create diagrams of the engine and electronic parts, and conclude by making a presentation to an elementary class about aerodynamics and the mechanical engineering necessary for flight.

One of the first steps in the process was the purchase of an inexpensive, small, light-weight plastic RC plane. It arrived early in the week, and after spending a couple of days figuring out how to put it together and reading the owner's manual, the day for its inaugural flight arrived. At least, that's what the boys were hoping.

Tamara always tells all of the students that obstacles will be a part of the process in their independent projects. She has been teaching gifted students long enough to know that everyone hits bumps in the road, though some hit bigger bumps than others. The younger kids tend not to believe her on this, but soon enough they realize that they, too, will have to overcome some obstacles in order to complete their project or study.

Ford and Lew spent 30 minutes trying to get their plane off the ground with absolutely no success. It would taxi around the parking lot outside Tamara's classroom window, turn and stop, and go forward again, but never once did it get a wheel off the ground. Persistence, Tamara tells her students, is what breeds success. They, too, have heard of Thomas Edison, and they know he tried over 1,000 times before finally finding a way to make a lightbulb that could be mass-reproduced for use by the "ordinary person" outside of a scientific laboratory. They also know that when a reporter once asked Edison how he felt about failing 1,000 times in his attempt to make a lightbulb, he replied that he had not failed 1,000 times; rather, he had successfully found 1,000 ways how *not* to make a lightbulb.

Persistence hadn't paid off yet for Lew and Ford. They came inside, frustrated and spent. Looking at the clock, they realized that their class was nearly over. They sat down to discuss possible options. They approached Tamara to ask if they could go back outside and try "one more time." With only five minutes left of class and knowing that the plane hadn't been anywhere near working just a short time ago, she told them to go ahead. She didn't think it would work, so she wasn't worried about the time. She should have known better.

Marcus and Haiden were already cleaned up and so went outside with the two boys to help. Tamara and the other students watched from the windows. Marcus picked the plane up, and Ford revved up the controls.

Tamara also tells her students that positive risk-taking is often an essential element to success and to overcoming obstacles. It soon became apparent that this was the new strategy.

Marcus leaned backward and heaved the plane upward with all his might, throwing it toward the sky with muscle-created lift. The plane rose, then drifted down toward the grass, tipping its nose up, then down, then sideways. Ford grappled with the controls, trying to figure out the best formula for saving the plane from grass stains. Lew stood nearby, tense with anticipation and dread. Haiden paced back and forth, flapping his arms like a bird, as if to will it into flight.

Then, just when it seemed all hope was lost, the plane lifted up and soared! A cheer went up among the students watching with Tamara from inside. The plane raced toward the fence at the edge of the school's property, aiming to surprise the cattle grazing peacefully on the other side. "Bring it back, Ford!" Tamara hollered through the window's screen. "If it crashes over there, it'll take all afternoon to find it and bring it back!" She particularly didn't want to tangle with the gigantic black bull in one of the fields.

Ford was so excited that the plane was finally flying that he'd forgotten to keep his hands on the controls. Struggling with them once again, he managed to turn the flying object around and bring it safely back over the fence.

"Okay, Ford, the bell rang. Bring it in for a landing."

He must've been aiming to land the little plane on the sidewalk, but he was still struggling with how to exert the right amount of pressure on the controls. He turned the plane around and brought it in lower to the ground, but the plane was faster in the air than Ford was on his feet. It passed him by, going behind him, and he didn't turn around in time to see it heading right for Marcus and Haiden. Marcus arched his back, and the little plane passed through where his belly had been. Ford turned around just in time to see it aiming right for Haiden. Perhaps Haiden thought Ford would control it away from him, because he became a bullfighter in front of the plane, daring it to come at him. He soon realized, though, that Ford didn't yet know enough about the controls and that just as he had dared, the plane was coming right at him. As the plane approached low to the ground, Haiden leaned backwards and kept leaning until he'd fallen flat on his back, just in time for the little plane to glide right over the top of his body.

As teachers, we've all had moments like these when our teaching careers flash before our eyes. The students inside roared with laughter, and Haiden bounced up, ready to take on the plane again. Ford finally managed to bring it safely to the ground, and everyone left for their next class. As he was cleaning up and putting the plane away, the enthusiasm emanating from Ford was palpable. This was a boy who rarely smiled, and yet he was positively giddy with excitement. "Well, I guess we might be able to do something with this plane after all, Miss Fisher," he said. Yes indeed, Ford. Yes, indeed.

Tamara left work that day with a feeling of satisfaction regarding what appeared to be wonderful progress for Lew and Ford. They saw their project all the way through to an exhilarating finish.

Sometimes the students need to learn to persist even when things go awry. Other times they need encouragement or support to persist and go the extra mile. For her sixth-grade language arts class, Mrs. Lopez assigns the students to write a short story. Leah, also a student in Tamara's GT class, had filled half of a spiral notebook by the due date. Her "short" story was an incredible fantasy that used amazing symbolism. Leah asked Mrs. Lopez if she could continue beyond the due date to turn it into a novel. Mrs. Lopez of course agreed. For the rest of the year, during any moment of free time, Leah would continue working on her story. Occasionally she would ask Mrs. Lopez questions like, "Do you know what the universal symbol for truth is?" A great combination of challenge and her own strengthening persistence, this opportunity was just what Leah's creative mind needed.

Every gifted child deserves challenge—the opportunity to learn persistence and hard work. There are also times when the challenge is not the student's alone. Sometimes persistence takes two.

In Mrs. Leon's third-grade class, there was a young man who loved dinosaurs. Mrs. McGillicuddy was working as a weekly mentor with him and decided that raising triops shrimp might catch his interest, as they are a species of shrimp that have survived hundreds of millions of years and represent what might be considered a dinosaur culture, though we're sure that some dinosaur somewhere would take offense to that. They live a short period of time and lay eggs in the sand. The eggs can survive for years, even after the sand dries out. Mrs. Leon agreed to let the boy raise his triops in her classroom, as he needed to watch and care for them every day. She didn't have a problem with it.

So Mrs. McGillicuddy found some triops eggs and had the student do some research on the Internet. They found a huge container that would hold water and set up the habitat inside. What they didn't realize was that triops are stinky and dirty, even when their water is changed often. By the time they were about an inch long and looking like bullfrog tadpoles, the water smelled so bad that the teacher had a headache every day. But even though she was living with this mucky, smelly stuff growing in the back of her classroom, she went along with it for the student's sake.

The situation became more tense as the largest triop turned cannibalistic and began eating the smaller triops. Of course, that upset the student. *The Very Hungry Triop*. That title wouldn't make such a great picture book for some young readers.

The teacher, while feeling empathy for the boy, was also admittedly very excited when the project was almost over, as there was only one large-ish triop left, and finally even that one died.

However, leave it to Mrs. McGillicuddy to see still more learning opportunities. Next, she convinced the teacher to let the student carefully bail the water out of the container and leave the sand to dry, just in case the triops had laid eggs in the sand. "Just think, you could grow your own in class next year!"

Lovely thought.

So the sand sat in the class for another month as it slowly dried. Finally the teacher couldn't take it anymore. The sand had to go. Sometimes, even the hardiest person can only be so persistent before sanity is tested and olfactory nerves revolt.

And thus, this also brings us to another point of wisdom. One of the other tricks of teaching kids persistence is helping them to know when to quit. "Never surrender, never give up" is a great slogan *most* of the time, but there *are* some occasions when giving up is an okay thing to do. Sometimes, it's downright necessary. Sometimes, enough is enough.

The same is true in relationships. As we discussed earlier, gifted kids tend to be intense, and sometimes their intensity gets in the way of their ability to read other people's feelings. Louie may be a tease, and he may be good at it, but when Micayla says, "Stop it!" Louie needs to learn to respect her feelings. Or when a teacher has really and truly reached the end of the infamous rope, she needs to be able to say, "That's enough," and Louie needs to learn that "enough" means enough.

There may be other occasions when the goal a child is pursuing is not a positive one. Perhaps Louie is causing himself harm by persisting in dwelling on a hurtful event in his past, and it's time for him to move on. He may need help with this. He may even need *persistent* help with this.

But when it comes to a kid who wants to pursue her passions or her dreams, that student needs to be encouraged to keep going. She needs to learn to deal with and overcome discouraging obstacles. A teacher shouldn't make the process so easy that the student doesn't have to work for it. The Olympics inspire us all because we see people who've worked tremendously hard succeed in accomplishing the amazing. We wouldn't be so engaged in watching if the bar were set too low and athletes didn't have to stretch their own limits in the process.

And while natural and necessary challenges should be present, a teacher should be paving the way to achieving the goals of the child, not constructing unnecessary speed bumps. Please, no busywork. Please. Gifted kids don't need it. We heard of one high school teacher who sent a letter home saying that yes, she did give busywork to the students. After all, wasn't that part of life? Wouldn't there be busywork at home or at the office? Well, imagine an employer who gave unnecessary work to his employees just to keep them busy. Doesn't sound like there would be much profit in that, does there? And for goodness sake, we don't know of anyone who washes dishes just for the enjoyment of it. Usually it only happens because the dishes *need* to be washed.

So make every assignment, every task, every challenge worth the effort it takes to get it done. Give the child a *reason* to persist. And when it comes to a child learning how to persist through those less pleasant yet necessary tasks—otherwise known as challenges—it's a teacher's job to encourage, support, and set reasonably high expectations for the child. Just as important, it's the teacher's job to make sure the *necessary* challenges are there.

Vicky loves her second-grade class. She loves her teacher. She brings home 100% marks on most of her papers. Everything seems peachy on the surface. But if asked, she'll tell you she's bored. In her own words, "I wish the work was harder. I want to learn something!"

We hope she'll run into a few difficult situations that will help her to learn to overcome and not get discouraged so that, little by little, her brain and her persistence muscles will get an increasingly difficult workout. Otherwise, if she gets hit with a huge challenge all of a sudden in a high school AP class or in college, she won't be mentally or emotionally prepared to tackle difficult tasks and stick with them.

By her freshman year in high school, Hope had taken Tamara's Advanced Studies class twice. It's a good thing, too, because her project her freshman year required a healthy dose of that strengthened persistency. Hope wanted to learn about Braille[16]—and not just learn about it, but also learn how to read it. The high school had a blind student, Coby, and a special teacher who helped him by translating assignments and other materials using a computerized Braille machine that the district had purchased many years before when Coby was in elementary school. Mrs. Chang had been his teacher aide for about 10 years, so she knew a lot about Braille. She graciously agreed to help Hope with her project.

After Mrs. Chang had taught her just the basic Braille alphabet, Hope asked if she could take a sample home to practice. So Mrs. Chang printed three pages of Coby's U.S. history notes in Braille and gave them to Hope to take home. Hope didn't have a translated print copy of the Braille notes, so she had no idea what they actually said. Mrs. Chang had thought Hope would just try translating a couple of lines, but the next day, Hope came to school with all of the pages neatly interlined. Interlining is when the words are printed above the Braille. Hope mentioned how frustrating it had been and how she had stayed up all night working on it. "Are you sure you gave me the whole alphabet?"

It dawned on Mrs. Chang that the Braille computer writes out words that are contracted, sort of like a shorthand or code. The notes that Hope had translated hadn't been in words after all but rather were in this Braille version of code.

That Hope had been able to translate three pages of Braille notes while only knowing the alphabet meant that she'd had to use context clues and trial and error to figure out the code for Braille words. This is amazingly difficult! Yet she had done it.

It took persistence. And persistence was something Hope had.

Help the kids to develop their persistency muscles. Consider the classroom a mental workout room—a brain gym. You wouldn't ask little Arnold Schwarzenegger to start out with five pound ankle weights just because that's what the rest of the class is using, would you? If he didn't get more of a challenge than that, he would lose what he already had. Give them something that pushes them a little and teaches them that they are capable so that they can accomplish whatever they choose to accomplish in their lives. Help them to learn how to harness that energy and muscle power so that they can use it wisely. Encourage them to continue to be persistent if there is something that they really want to achieve.

"Opportunity is missed by most people, because it is dressed in overalls and looks like work." That's just one more bit of wisdom from Thomas Edison, Mr. Persistence himself. The man knew what he was talking about.

9: Sensitivity

> *"If I can stop one heart from breaking,*
> *I shall not live in vain;*
> *If I can ease one life the aching,*
> *Or cool one pain,*
> *Or help one fainting robin*
> *Into his nest again,*
> *I shall not live in vain."*
> ~ Emily Dickinson ~

Emily Dickinson[17] was a peculiar person. There's no doubt about that. She was also a brilliant person. No doubt about that, either. And to take it further, there's no doubt that when she wrote this poem, she was feeling what many gifted children experience every day. She knew what it was like to be highly sensitive—probably more so than most people. Her poems illustrate her physical, environmental, and emotional sensitivity.

Gifted children do experience high levels of sensitivity in many different areas, and it often sets them apart from those around them. They can smell things that others can't smell. They see and notice things others can't see. They can feel things others can't feel. Really. Their five senses all seem to operate in a state of hyper-vigilance. Too often, the adults in their lives discount those hyper-senses as the child being overly dramatic, doing something just for attention, or having an overactive imagination. If their sensitivities are written off and invalidated, gifted children may feel isolated. They get the message, "You may only sense what the rest of us are sensing, because anything beyond that is impossible and absurd."

Because gifted children are highly sensitive to the world around them, they notice details others miss. They see the ordinary with new eyes. They worry about problems in their communities and around the world, and they'll try to do something to fix those problems, too. They're sensitive to the thoughts and feelings of others, and they're sensitive to nuances in communication—both verbal and nonverbal. They can pinpoint how the teacher feels by just walking into the room. The hum of the fluorescent lights in the classroom can drive them up the wall, while the rest of the class works away without noticing the high-pitched buzz above their heads. They may offer help to another student before that other student asks because they can see a need before someone else brings it to their attention.

The light switch in the annex to Tamara's classroom is a bit larger than most and controls the motion-sensored lights in that space. It also emits a barely audible high-pitched squeal, rendering many of her gifted students unable to work in that room.

A cook at Tamara's middle school makes delicious soups, but one soup in particular uses a variety of strong spices whose odor wafts down the hallways outside the cafeteria. The entire gymnasium is between her classroom and the cafeteria, but nonetheless, Tamara makes a point to keep her classroom door closed on vegetable beef soup days because otherwise, the odor from the spices leaves many of her students sneezing and sniffling from the assault on their sinuses.

Gifted children often experience irritation from their hair or clothing. Most children do not insist, as Emily Dickinson supposedly did, on wearing all white all of the time. But they do have clothing issues. Tags scratch and rub. Hair tickles. Wrinkles pinch. Socks or shoes irritate. As an adult, it is often easier to tell the child to "buck up" than it is to solve the problem. As a result, the child may spend an entire day fidgeting in discomfort and focused on the irritant, whatever it is, sometimes in pain—a pain incomprehensible to the rest of the world, but very real to her. Then we wonder why she isn't doing well in school and why she can't focus on her schoolwork. Of course, we can't let them run around stark naked because their clothes bother them, but we can be a bit flexible now and then. We can cut the tags out of their clothing (don't let the second graders do this themselves unless you want them to wear holy clothing!) and turn their socks inside out so the seams don't tickle their toes. Who really cares if their socks are inside out?

A fourth-grade student approached the teacher and said, "My feet can't breathe." Fortunately, her teacher took her seriously and told the little girl that she was allowed to sit in class without wearing her shoes. The teacher figured it was a small price to pay to allow the girl to be comfortable enough to focus her attention elsewhere—maybe even on her work.

Gifted children may also experience high levels of sensitivity when it comes to their feelings or those of others. Karen's six-year-old son Rupert displays unexpected outbursts now and then that betray a highly sensitive nature. One day when Karen's daughter Magnolia, who is 14, was trying to be a supportive big sister and encourage Rupert in his current love of school, she accidentally stepped on one of his sensitive spots. It was just before he went off to school one day, and he was in the middle of a peanut butter and honey sandwich. Magnolia said, "Rupert, it's a good thing you're going to school, because if you didn't, you'd be dumb."

Rupert was incensed. He jumped from his stool and shouted at her, "*What?* Are you saying that before I was old enough to go to school, I was *dumb?*" The thought horrified him.

Keep in mind that Rupert is usually an easy-going kid.

Rupert is sensitive and careful about other people's feelings. He has been known to give up something he wants in order to spare the feelings of a sibling or friend. If his friend wants one of his toys, Rupert will give it to him. If he knows that his dad is exhausted after a long day at work, Rupert will tell him, "That's okay. You don't have to take me for an ice cream cone tonight." If someone else is being picked on, he will immediately jump to that person's defense. And he says things like, "Mom, I don't think you're fat, and even if you are, I would never say that."

Rupert's family and friends greatly appreciate his sensitivity and caring.

A number of years ago, one of Tamara's students had a strong reaction to what she perceived to be an unjust environment created by a teacher in a regular classroom. Other students who had this teacher felt the same way she did, but Susanna truly suffered. She was so bothered by what she saw happening in the classroom—but couldn't control—that she developed an eye twitch, began losing hair, and even lost her lunch a few times in the classroom garbage can. To this day, hearing phrases that this teacher once used will send Susanna's eye a-quivering.

Like most young gifted children, Amanda is deeply concerned by what she sees on the news. She gets very upset, sometimes even sick to her stomach, when she watches news stories about people fighting or being killed. She internalizes the outside world's pain as if it were her own. Like Amanda, many gifted children have a strong reaction to conflict of any kind.

Bowen's best friend moved suddenly and without advance notice during the third grade when his parents divorced. When Bowen's mom explained to him that his friend wouldn't be returning, he replied, "If he is happy and doesn't have to listen to his parents fighting anymore, then I am happy for him. I will miss him, but I can call and write to him." This is pretty insightful and sensitive for a third grader.

Leigh participates every year in 4-H activities and usually raises a pig for her project. During a discussion about frustration one day in Tamara's class, Leigh commented that when she gets really frustrated, she goes to her pig and says, "Pork Chop, I've *had* it!"

Tamara said to her, "Oh, that's cute. You named your pig Pork Chop?"

Leigh replied, "No, I talk to him in the freezer. He *is* a pork chop!"

Okay, so, they do have their moments where practicality overrides the sensitivity issue.

Along with sensitivity, gifted children have a keen sense of justice, not only for themselves, but also for those around them.

A third grader, Angelina, came home from school every day in a foul mood. Her mother was perplexed, because this same child had loved school the previous year. In second grade, she earned near perfect scores in every subject, got up extra early for school every morning, and came home with a smile on her face. In third grade, she still brought home good grades, but her mood was something other than happy. When her mother asked her how she liked school, she said, "It's okay." When her mother asked how she liked her teacher, Angelina said, "Well, she's all right, I guess, but I feel bad for the students who don't do so well. She's really mean to them."

Angelina was experiencing both a strong sense of injustice and also deep empathy. The other students' pain was her pain. Empathy is another area of sensitivity that is often found in gifted children. While we don't want to deny the existence of *any* area of sensitivity that a child may be experiencing, when we run across a child who is experiencing extreme empathy, we want to encourage the healthy aspects of it and help the child find ways to relieve the anxiety they feel by looking for opportunities to relieve the suffering of those whose pain the child is feeling. We need to help children feel empowered that they can be problem solvers for themselves and for others.

When children worry about children in the world who are hungry or sick, they can raise money to send to the International Red Cross or other humanitarian aid organizations. When they are concerned about political issues, they can write to their elected representatives.

Consider Pearl S. Buck. She was not only an incredibly gifted author, but she also made landmark strides in the acceptance of child adoption. Her first biological child was mentally retarded, and after learning she could have no more children the natural way due to health problems, she went on to adopt seven other children. This personal experience with adoption spurred her passionate advocacy of its importance and possibilities. She started Welcome House®, the first international interracial adoption agency. She also founded the Pearl S. Buck International Foundation, which supports efforts to provide humanitarian assistance to needy children around the world. As the daughter of Presbyterian missionaries stationed in China, she spent her first 40 years living in China and later became an activist for citizenship for Chinese-Americans at a time when they were denied citizenship. She supported human rights initiatives that would give equal status to biracial children in many countries, as opposed to the social ostracism that often ruled their lives and kept them from opportunities. She obviously felt a great deal of empathy for children around the world who were in tough situations, and she acted on those strong feelings.

Another delightful aspect of sensitivity is the ability to recognize beauty in areas that most of the world might miss. Walter de la Mare wrote this about a snowflake:

Before I melt,
Come look at me!
This lovely icy filigree!

Atalanta, a student in a third grade class, snuck back inside soon after going out for recess one day. "Mr. Trinity, may I borrow a magnifying glass?"

"For recess?" her teacher asked.

"Yes, I want to look at the snowflakes falling on the playground."

What a gift it is to see so much beauty in the world! A high level of sensitivity is sometimes "irritating" (excuse the pun), but it also offers an opportunity to experience so much more than life appears to offer on the surface. It offers depth and richness.

Emily Dickinson's niece, Martha Dickinson Bianchi, wrote of her aunt, "She put more excitement into a dead fly than her neighbors got from a journey by stage-coach to Boston." Martha also said, "One may ask of the Sphinx, if life would not have been dearer to her, lived as other women would have lived it? Or if, in so doing and so being, she would have missed that inordinate compulsion, that inquisitive comprehension that made her Emily Dickinson?"

Sensitivity is a big part of who these gifted children are. They don't want to be changed, but they do want to know that someone believes them when they express their feelings. They may need to know that their sensitivity is real and valid. They don't need adults to discount or minimize their feelings.

A couple of years ago, Maria and four of Tamara's other students joined her for a presentation she was giving to all of the principals from the western region of Montana. The last half of the presentation was an opportunity for the principals to pose questions to the gifted students. One of them asked, "What would school be like for you if you didn't have the gifted program?"

Maria's response: "Without the gifted program, I think I would've jumped off a high place onto a hard one by now."

Because it was scary to hear such words come out of the mouth of a then-14-year-old, and knowing that *she* knew Maria was psychologically healthy but the principals did not, Tamara asked her to clarify for them what she meant.

"Well, I don't mean that literally, of course. It's just that that's how *frustrated* I would feel if I didn't have GT as an outlet. The regular classroom can be so stifling sometimes! GT gives me a place where I can be myself and where I can ponder all the weird things I want to research and think about."

Each child is unique, just like each snowflake. Teachers often work with a student for only one year, and then the next year, a whole new batch of unique snowflakes enters their classroom. After a decade or more of teaching, the accumulative avalanche of their faces can blur in their memories. It then becomes easy to lump students together into categories: "I have two ADHD students this year, one artist, three troublemakers, two shy kids, four with learning problems, two whose parents haven't taught them hygiene, and three who appear to be gifted, so at least I won't have to worry about *them*." After crossing paths with so many hundreds of kids, it can become easy to lose sight of their individual preciousness, despite our best intentions. Perhaps, when we notice our vision having narrowed like this, we can borrow a page from Atalanta: find a magnifying glass, take a closer look at each child, and tune into the unique talents, style, and potential of each one.

And what about the ones who are gifted—the students we teachers so often think we don't have to worry about? Remember, they are often plagued with their own worries. Their hypersensitive nature can leave them more vulnerable, more understanding, more worrisome, more perceptive, more depressed, more ecstatic, more irritated, more stress-prone, and more aware. While even scientific research (brain scans of gifted vs. average individuals) shows this sensitivity in the extra activity blazing in the gifted brains (read the article at www.newhorizons.org/spneeds/gifted/eide.htm), perhaps the best analogy comes from one such individual herself:

> *"The truly creative mind in any field is no more than this: A human creature born abnormally, inhumanly sensitive. To him…*
>
> *a touch is a blow,*
> *a sound is a noise,*
> *a misfortune is a tragedy,*
> *a joy is an ecstasy,*

a friend is a lover,
a lover is a god,
and failure is death.

"Add to this cruelly delicate organism the overpow-
ering necessity to create, create, create - - - so that
without the creating of music or poetry or books or
buildings or something of meaning, his very breath
is cut off from him. He must create, must pour out
creation. By some strange, unknown, inward
urgency he is not really alive unless he is creating."

~ Pearl S. Buck ~

Be aware of the possibilities of hypersensitivity in your classrooms. You may have to look for it. Some children will hide their feelings—either because they are shy or because their feelings have been denied them in the past. A child may be feeling a "funeral in his brain," to inaccurately quote Miss Emily, or experiencing a "sunset in a cup." Whatever the emotion, the irritant, the sensitivity, these children are entitled to their feelings, and some may want or need encouragement for coping with, expressing, or overcoming them.

10: Idealism

"We have it in our power to begin the world over again."
- Thomas Paine -

ave you ever known someone with big dreams? In particular, have you ever known someone with the drive and follow-through necessary to make those big dreams come true? These people are quite an inspiration, aren't they? They're also idealistic, another common feature of the gifted individual.

Throughout history, individuals with lofty goals and aspirations have encountered mixed levels of reception and success. From ridicule to support, from life-saving success to life-altering failure, their far-reaching attempts definitely get attention. It is those whose idealism lets them dare to dream big and who can back up their dreams with commitment that move human history forward with "one small step for man, one giant leap for mankind."

The founding fathers of America were perhaps among the biggest dreamers of all. What arrogance, what risk, what idealism, what ambition, what hope! To conceive of a new nation, structured in a new fashion, founded on a new collection of old and new principles is among the biggest dreams of human history. And because they dared to dream so big, hundreds of millions of people have since experienced freedom like nowhere else on earth, like no other time in history.

Big dreams cannot survive alone. Their sustenance is persistence, curiosity, creativity, intensity, attention to detail, divergent thinking, sensitivity, humility, and even the innocence of not knowing how much the odds may be stacked up against the vision. Big dreams are where it all comes together. As English poet Samuel Johnson said, "Your aspirations are your possibilities."

Big dreamers come in all shapes and sizes. They come from all parts of the world and from every background. Odds are, there are probably a few big dreamers in your classroom. Hopefully, you are one of them.

All students, but gifted students in particular, thrive under teachers who dream big. We're not talking about teachers who dream of every student achieving 100% on every test in every subject. That would imply that either the students are under an extreme amount of pressure or the work is too easy for them. We're talking about teachers who see limitless potential in those little brains, who see limitless potential in each subject, and who dream of bringing those subjects to life in a big way to help the information find a welcome and cozy home in those brains.

Sometimes, whether we realize it or not, we put limits on our students. We say, "Okay, this is what a first grader should know," or "This is what a fifth grader should know." We forget that all brain capacities and interest levels are not created equal.

A few years ago, Mrs. McGillicuddy did a pull-out program with a group of second and third graders. She determined what she wanted to study with them by simply deciding what it was that she, herself, wanted to learn more about. She liked bugs. So they studied bugs—entomology—and she learned right along with the kids as she went. She looked up everything she could find on the subject and gathered her own sources without going out to buy a bunch of books. She took the information and put it in a language the students could understand, yet she kept all of the technical names for the body parts, even though they were big words and appeared to be intimidating and beyond the students' age level. She figured that the kids understood and retained strange new words all of the time—words like "cafeteria." Not many children use that term at home. They don't ask their mothers for a snack and get sent to the cafeteria. And likewise, when they first start school, teachers don't say to them, "Okay, children, let's go down to the place where we eat food," or even "the kitchen." They say, "Line up to go to the cafeteria." The kids are okay with that. They can easily pick up on new terms they aren't familiar with.

Mrs. McGillicuddy drew a big picture of a grasshopper, laminated it, and made all of the labels to it. Little by little, the children began learning all of the scientific names for the body parts—not just *head, thorax,* and *abdomen,* but each section of the legs, mouths, and the rest, and how each insect compared with other insects. They studied a spider, and once they had that down, they compared spiders to insects. After that, they purchased some mealworms, because they were cheap to buy at the pet store. They were also cheap to raise—an all around cheap experiment. Mealworms are lowly creatures, especially when they start tunneling around in your flour bin. They have never been actively involved in keeping up with the Joneses.

The students used the mealworms to watch the metamorphosis of an insect. Each child was given some oatmeal, a slice of potato, and some larvae in a little plastic container. Each week they had to pick up the larva, which was difficult at first for some of them, but because they knew they were scientists, they overcame their squeamishness. They had to measure their larvae, look at the tiny legs underneath, and draw pictures of them. In the meantime, while the larvae were busy growing, the students worked on butterfly reports.

The students became so attached to their larvae that after the experiment was over, they wanted to take them home. Mrs. McGillicuddy received several phone calls from parents who asked, "At what point can we get rid of these things?" because the kids had learned how to keep them alive, and they were beginning to multiply and prosper in their little containers. Not a pleasant thought, as far as most people were concerned.

At the end of the unit, Mrs. McGillicuddy gave the young entomologists a test that covered all of the body parts and the other things they'd studied. The test was two pages long and included fill-in-the-blank and matching problems. She was determined that they were going to pass it before they moved on to something else. By "passing," she meant something above 90%. There were 17 students, and all but five passed it the first time. She took a few more days to study with those five and tested them again. All but two passed. So she studied with those two for a few more days until they passed. She said that the students who didn't do as well were the students who were extremely bright but didn't know how to study because they'd never had to before. They'd never been challenged in their schoolwork.

Next, Mrs. McGillicuddy decided she would take the tests over to show to the high school biology teacher. She said, "This is a test that some of my second and third graders just took on our entomology unit."

The teacher looked at the tests and said, "*How* old?"

"Second and third grade."

"*They* did this?" he asked. Then he said, "This test is what I would give my tenth graders." He couldn't believe that seven- and eight-year-old kids had passed this test with a 90 or above score. Challenge! These kids like to learn, and they like challenge. Mrs. McGillicuddy explained to him that they were interested and they were capable, so there wasn't any reason not to give them the information.

He looked at the tests again and said, "Now what am I going to do with them when *I* get them?"

Which just goes to show what kids can do when they're given a chance, when information and knowledge isn't "saved for later" or withheld from them because it's not scheduled for their brains on that particular grade level.

Schools are all wrong when they say, kindergarteners must know this but not that. Third graders must know that but not this. These are the rules. This is tradition! It's the way we've always done it here. The decisions have been made. Teachers of the gifted who are on their way to becoming gifted teachers realize this and are willing to be flexible when a child requires it.

Big dreamers are sometimes the students, and all they really need is a little bit of guidance to help place a firm foundation beneath their dreams.

One teacher had a second grader in class who was fascinated with airplanes. We'll call him Charles L. (as in Lindbergh). Thankfully, his teacher saw Charles's fascination as a way for him to learn about more than planes. She let him run with his ideas and gave him the freedom to work on a project of his choosing. He decided to design an airplane contest for his class. He made every model airplane in the book that he had. He then designed different contests for the planes to compete in, such as which plane was the fastest, the slowest, the sleekest, the most acrobatic, etc. He had all of his information organized on a clipboard. His mom and his teacher went with him to the cafeteria to make the arrangements to use the room, and they let him do all the talking and arranging. When the day came, they sat there and watched for two hours while each of the kids was given a plane and then went through the competition. At the end, this young man gave everyone a ribbon of his own making. It was important to him that everyone had ribbons so no one would feel bad.

Okay, so what did Charles L. gain from this? Well, he used his reading and comprehension skills, not to mention small-motor coordination, to build the models. He used organizational skills designing an activity that might stress out the average adult. He exercised his creative thinking abilities in the planning of the competitions. He found himself in a real-life situation dealing with people where he chose to be thoughtful and compassionate, not because that was the assignment or the weekly getting-along skill, but because he knew it was the right thing to do. He had natural leadership skills.

Not bad for a second grader. And all of this was accomplished without lesson plans or tests or worksheets. Just teacher flexibility.

What did the other kids gain from this? A really fun afternoon? Yep. And they also saw a kid their age do something big and smart and organized. At least some of them had to realize that seven-year-olds are more capable than they had previously been led to believe. They got a little taste of their own potential.

Allowing children the chance to taste their own potential requires certain sacrifices and attitude changes from teachers and parents. How often has a child been prevented from learning something new because the teacher said, "You'll be learning about that next year." How often has a child been prevented from conducting a great learning experiment because Mom or Dad said, "It'll make too big of a mess." *Why are we always putting roadblocks in the way of our children?*

Yes, there do need to be some rules and restrictions for reasons of safety and reality, but let's not quash so many of their dreams and curiosities simply because of the inconveniences to ourselves. What a tragedy it will be for our society if we continue to do so. Children are capable of more than they know— and of more than *we* know. But in order to find out just how far they can go, we must take a chance on them and let them take some chances, too.

"Someday I'm going to be the editor of my own magazine," Audrey said to Tamara one day when she was in the sixth grade, not long after Tamara met her and had become her GT teacher. She didn't have to wait long. The very next year, she did just that through the Advanced Studies class at the middle school.

Frustrated that all of the teen magazines available to her were superficial, skimpy, and over-done, Audrey decided to create and produce Volume I of her own magazine, *Limited*. She ventured into the realm of celebrity interviews, peer surveys, product reviews, and magazine production. This beautiful accomplishment drew upon and fine-tuned her skills in writing, organization, problem solving, communication, and technology. The next year, in eighth grade, Volume II was eagerly anticipated by classmates and was greeted with awe and enthusiasm by all who read it. Through Volume II, Audrey further polished the skills she had developed on Volume I, plus she enhanced the magazine with some key improvements, such as using glossy paper for printing it and securing an *exclusive* interview with one of the most famous celebrities of that year.

Audrey used the two years after the publication of her first volumes to learn a tremendous amount about layout and journalism. She took every journalism course available at her high school. She served as editor for the high school's national award-winning school newspaper, and she succeeded in securing many contacts in the world of publishing, including regular email contact with the then-editor of *CosmoGIRL*! While in high school, Audrey contributed to nine national teen magazines, many of them multiple times. She served as a reader contributor for three of the publications, including getting two-year contracts with two of the magazines. She became as adept in the complex magazine world as other bright teens are with computers. The depth and breadth of her knowledge, curiosity, and accomplishments in the field was truly astounding and rivaled that of graduate students in journalism.

Following those two years of further learning were two years of creating Volume III, now appropriately re-titled *UnLimited*. From the articles to the printing, the creative layout to the understanding zeal within its pages, it is as close to professional quality as one can imagine. Everyone who reads it is stunned that it was a one-person production and done by a high school student rather than an entire magazine staff. You can check it out yourself at www.polson.k12.mt.us/salishian/current/02-03/magazine-web.pdf.

There were many hurdles to overcome and plenty of opportunities to tell Audrey that she might have to settle for something less than her original vision. The printing alone was a huge obstacle. Sending her magazine to a professional printer would have cost thousands of dollars and therefore was financially out of the reach of both her and the school. Yet she wasn't willing to settle for photocopies or even general quality printouts. After investigating all possibilities, both on and off campus, she managed to convince the high school's administration that the project was worthy of the school's newest and biggest printer. Despite the costs of ink and paper, the district allowed the printing of over 200 copies of *UnLimited*. Audrey's big dream was realized.

We've got to quit telling our idealistic big dreamers, "You can't," "You'll never," "Impossible," "No way," "Scale it down," "Be realistic," "Try something a little easier," or "You'd better stay with the class." Instead, let's say to them, "It's worth a try," "You've run into a problem? What are you going to do about it?" "Anything is possible," "You'll never know until you ask," "Don't assume that it can't happen," or "How much do you want this?"

Audrey worked harder on her magazine than Tamara ever imagined possible when she first opened the door to such open-ended possibilities for her students. When Tamara gives presentations to local, state, and national groups of teachers about her Advanced Studies course, the magazine is consistently the most impressive and memorable example that she brings. It is a hit because Audrey's magazine, "for teens, by a teen," is just what teen magazines should be—insightful, real, thought-provoking, innovative, genuine, and a true class act.

In this course designed to promote independent learning skills, Audrey far surpassed Tamara's hopes and expectations. She dreamed big, and she made it happen. Now in college, majoring in journalism, Audrey continues to create avenues of opportunity that will help her fulfill her big dreams, including securing a hard-to-win summer internship with *Seventeen* magazine.

Big dreams can be set into motion by the most unlikely events. Tamara's student Maria fell off her bicycle at "high speed" when she was in first grade. A trip to the doctor's office to check her wounds provides a great story about Maria's innate curiosities.

While the nurse was picking the imbedded pebbles out of the skin of Maria's leg, Maria tried to convince her to let her keep the rocks. A budding geologist? Nope. She wanted to see what would happen to the blood on them over time. A budding scientist. You read about her Western Blotting experiments earlier. Well, here's the rest of the story.

Microbes fascinate Maria to this day. She considers it a challenge from nature to see which substances she can get microbes to grow on. She nurtures these specimens with the same tender, loving care that others give to their pets. Most of her multitude of experiments are hidden in her family's basement, but once she hid her research in a butter box in the refrigerator. That was a great hiding place for her cold-temperature experiments, until the fateful day that a family friend came over for dinner, opened the box and saw what was inside, and quickly threw it away, not knowing the actual significance of the growth within. Imagine the neighbor's shock when she found that grisly surprise! And imagine Maria's horror at losing a well-tended experiment to such a fate!

Maria's penchant for collecting samples from unusual sources has created some notoriety for her in her small community. Another student left a solution of paper maché in Tamara's classroom cabinet over the weekend once, and on Monday morning, Maria joyfully scooped off the thick mold covering it. The refrigerator in the teachers' lounge has coughed up many a great specimen. And one day, Maria just happened to be near the nurse's office soon after another student had lost his lunch. Yep, that became a sample source, too.

Maria has taken Tamara's Advanced Studies class for each of the past five years. In seventh grade, her project consisted of a series of dissections of animal organs donated by local butcher shops. Her first question when calling the butcher shop to request leftovers was always, "Can I please have your liver?" They gave her pig lungs and hearts, as well as cow livers, hearts, kidneys, esophagi, and intestines. Tamara has a small, dorm-sized fridge in her middle school classroom where Maria stored many of these biological specimens. Most would be placed there in the morning while Tamara was at another school. She never quite knew what to expect when opening that door. Imagine her surprise one day when she opened it to find a pair of cow eyeballs staring back at her!

During class, Maria would dissect these bloody gems while the other students worked on their projects, too. They graciously gave her a table all to herself! She tried growing the same mold sample on the pig heart and the cow heart to see how each specimen's tissue dealt with the same fungus growth. One of the boys in the class that semester, Keefe, was creating a student newspaper for the school. One article was boldly titled, "Tell Tale Heart Found Beating in Miss Fisher's Classroom!"

Later that year, Maria's middle school had a 1950s Talent Show. While the other students showcased talents of singing and dance, Maria instead demonstrated for the whole school a heart dissection, in honor of the first heart pacemaker developed in the 1950s. She chose a beef heart for her presentation because it was large enough to be seen by the whole audience. Assisting her on stage was her friend Max, whom she insisted had to sit "Second Scalpel" for the show.

A few weeks later on a sunny Saturday afternoon, Tamara received a phone call from Maria:

"Miss Fisher, can Max and I come over and dissect a calf brain at your house? My mom doesn't want it in her house, and Max's mom would totally freak."

"Well, I'd have some ground rules…," Tamara said.

"Oh, we expected that; we'll abide by whatever rules you want to set."

Tamara confirmed with their parents that they were okay with the students coming over, and then she laid out her ground rules. Half an hour later, the students arrived with the brain and set up shop on her kitchen table (thickly protected with several layers of garbage bags). It turns out that all of Maria's requests for leftovers from the local butcher shops had made quite a name for her among the local meat tenders. A valley rancher had a calf born that morning with severe physical deformities, to a degree that the calf would soon die a painful death if not euthanized. From the rancher to the vet to the butcher, and then into the hands of a future neurosurgeon, came a fresh specimen of the rarest kind. Maria was ecstatic and glowing with anticipation. Max was a bit green around the gills but equally curious.

After moving on to high school, Maria was able to take advantage of a great summer opportunity that matches exceptional high school students with a university mentor (www.gifted.uconn.edu/mentoruc.html). Through her experiences there, she was able to expand her skills and knowledge in scientific research far beyond what she had expected. As part of her work in the lab at the "Brain Power" site, she participated side-by-side with professors and graduate students as they studied certain neurological disorders and their possible origins. Each day after her hours at the lab, Maria would call Tamara up and gush about what an amazing day it had been. "It can't possibly get any better than this," she would say. But then the next day would out-do the day before, and once again she would proclaim that it couldn't get any better. It consistently did, though. Tamara found herself surprised and amazed with the degree of involvement Maria was afforded in the lab. She had certainly supposed that such an experience would be hands-on and in-depth for Maria, but the level to which she was actually involved was truly incredible. Those at the lab stretched her great pre-existing scientific skills and set her onto a whole new plane of knowledge and ability. Having now used a fluorescent microscope, for example, no "merely regular" microscope in her small town cuts mustard for Maria anymore. Maria lives life to its fullest when she is up to her elbows (literally and figuratively) in science, anatomy, and experimentation. And of course, she dreams about doing even more!

Now that her sister is away at college, Maria has transformed the older girl's bedroom into a laboratory, complete with red lights, ventilation system, centrifuge, vortex, and an electrophoresis machine. The electrophoresis machine is where the electricity comes from to move the proteins through the gel in a Western Blotting experiment. Weekends and late nights find her there, making big dreams come true. She also knows how to use the electrophoresis machine to run a DNA sample and recently conducted an experiment with the intent of proving or disproving a hypothesis of hers.

Perhaps you have seen an episode or two of the TV show *CSI*[18] ("Crime Scene Investigation"), in which the characters are crime scene investigators who utilize their scientific skills and knowledge to solve crimes. The images they show of the separate genes in DNA (the little fuzzy bars lined up) are generated through electrophoresis. Well, when this is done in the real world, one of the bars always comes out fuzzier than the others, with a bit of a "pinch" in the middle. While most scientists believe it to be one gene, there has been some question as to whether it could actually be two genes. Because she is willing to let herself dream big, Maria wanted to prove whether it is one or two genes. Through her summer experience and vast amount of reading in the field, she became aware of a particular substance that, when used during electrophoresis, helps to clarify and better define each bar of the DNA profile. To her knowledge, no one had yet used it to clarify this gene (or pair of genes). So Maria aspired to do so herself.

Herein enters an obstacle: Where could she get the needed five microliters of this substance? Five microliters are about equal to the size of this line: _____. A vial of that amount of the substance costs, on average, about $3,000, and it must be kept on dry ice to maintain a certain cold temperature. How many of us are giving up already? Not Maria! Suffice it to say, she found a laboratory (with the help of a friend who is a research scientist) that was willing to "lose" a vial so that she could conduct her experiment. It arrived over spring break, when she would have many consecutive hours available to pursue her hypothesis. The results? Well, it clarified one single gene. Maria was disappointed, because had it been two as she had hoped, she certainly would've caused some ripples in the scientific community. Nonetheless, her willingness to dream big and see her idealism through is now an even stronger facet of her personality.

In our view, encouraging the highly unusual interests of gifted children is imperative. Think of all of the bright kids in our nation whose deep curiosities and big dreams are crushed by rule-tidy parents and teachers who fear what to them is an unknown or who need to control every aspect of the child's play and learning.

Read through the biographies of eminent individuals who have made significant positive contributions to the world and you will find elements of risk and playful exploration in their big dreams, both in their childhoods and in their adult lives. Alexander Fleming, who famously, and accidentally, discovered the mold from which we get penicillin, used to "paint" with molds and bacteria. He knew which ones grew in each color and how fast; with this knowledge, he could prep a Petri dish and a few days later have a fairly detailed picture of a house or a balle-rina. His "play" in his field was a part of what helped him make his great discovery because it helped him remain finely tuned to the attributes of the specimens that other scientists might have overlooked as irrelevant.

Who would have thought that painting with molds and bacteria would ever amount to anything serious, let alone a dis-covery that has saved untold numbers of lives? Thankfully, Mr.

Fleming was persistent in pursuing his interests, in spite of its oddness—and probable low sale value in the art world. And think about it—while other scientists were seriously at work, Fleming was doodling in Petri dishes.

Now, imagine a student in your own classroom who flies a bit off the mark, or who imagines big, impossible dreams, or who seems determined to devote a large portion of his time pursuing things that seem irrelevant to most people. Perhaps, instead of squelching interests and dreams that we don't understand, we ought to be looking for ways to open doors, to incorporate those interests into daily work, or to provide other opportunities that will set the little brains free to explore the worlds of their own choosing.

We don't always know who we're working with, really. We're just seeing little seedlings in the beginning stages of their lives. We can't predict which child, if allowed to do so, will change the world, save millions of lives, bring hope to the hopeless, or figure out how to mass produce more efficient transportation.

Built on the visions of big dreamers, America, though it has its imperfections, is a beacon of freedom to the rest of the world, because the founding fathers and mothers were willing to *dream big*. Hundreds, perhaps thousands, of people risk their lives *every day* to come here and pursue dreams of their own. While that fact creates a controversy of its own, it is also a testament to the power of that dream devised 200+ years ago. "A constitution founded on these principles introduces knowledge among the people, and inspires them with a conscious dignity, becoming freemen." John Adams and the others were visionaries, willing to set a tremendously lofty goal and risk everything to get there, benefiting in the end the life, liberty, and happiness of millions. Why, then, do we in this great country often discourage the young big dreamers among us from following a similar path? Do we not understand the importance of idealism's potential outcomes?

Children like Maria and Audrey need to be encouraged because every day they face a peer culture and a society that often do not understand them. They are ridiculed for being interested in "weird" things, they are told they're crazy for wanting to experiment and play with such oddities, and they're put down for not being "normal." Each child like Audrey or Maria needs someone to let him know that these "oddities" are actually precious commodities. Our world *needs* people who glow with excitement over things that many other people would turn their noses up at.

It's time to open our minds to new possibilities, to be big dreamers ourselves, and to encourage big dreamers in young bodies to realize their potential. It's not only the right thing to do, but who knows—some day they may tell the world in their Nobel Peace Prize acceptance speech that they owe it all to a teacher who let them dream big—and that teacher might be you!

11: Humility

"Whatever you are, be a good one."
~ Abraham Lincoln ~

Associating humility with gifted children may seem para-doxical to some readers. After all, each of us can probably think of a talented individual we know who has a rather arrogant attitude and high opinion of himself—so high, in fact, that those around him grow weary of hearing him spell out just how much he knows about a certain topic (especially when it's quite a bit more than you really wanted to know) or hearing about his many accomplishments. But of those people who actually rise to some level of success, of people who make significant positive contributions to society, a corresponding degree of humility is often found. The humility stems from the knowledge and realization of just how much one *doesn't* know, just how much one *hasn't* accomplished, and just how much more there is to do in the world.

Anyone who specializes in a field can attest to the fact that the more you know about the field, the more you realize you actually don't know. As one question is answered, more are inevitably formed. Research scientists live and die by this fact of life. But they keep going. Most people who are truly at the top of their game and eminent in their fields are humble enough to recognize the deficits in their knowledge. Yet they still have the confidence to push forward, to aim higher.

Can confidence and humility coexist? Of course. It is arrogance and humility that fight for space in the same room. Confidence and humility, on the other hand, can strengthen one another. They are opposite sides of the same coin.

Abraham Lincoln was confident enough to try for some pretty lofty goals in his lifetime, yet he was also humble enough to recognize his perceived and actual failings: "Nobody has ever expected me to be President. In my poor, lean, lank face, nobody has ever seen that any cabbages were sprouting." Lincoln wisely used his humility as a strength. In 1860, when he ran for President the first time, Lincoln received a letter from an 11-year-old girl named Grace Bedell in which she hypothesized that if he grew a beard, more women would find him appealing and would therefore try to convince their husbands to vote for him. Anyone with large amounts of arrogance probably would not have even bothered to read a letter from a little girl in the first place. But Lincoln, willing to consider viable alternatives, not only wrote back, he actually took the young girl's advice. He grew a beard for the first time in his life! By the time he was inaugurated, he had sprouted the characteristic beard everyone now associates with him.

But how do we help gifted children develop a balance of confidence and humility? Some gifted children will need to develop more confidence in their own abilities, while other will need to learn to place a higher value on the abilities of others. Some gifted children will be meek and humble, while others will not only be aware of their extraordinary abilities, they will broadcast that fact to anyone who'll listen—and to everyone else who doesn't want to hear it anymore.

Adelle, a first grader, was well aware of her intelligence. She made it clear that she knew she was above her peers on every level. Her parents had invested their dreams and ambitions into this only child. They praised her abilities; they could talk about nothing else. In short, it wasn't necessarily the child's fault that she was so full-of-herself arrogant. Rather than a sense of self-worth, her parents had instilled a sense of superiority in her. She wasn't valuable for herself—she was only valuable because she was superior to those around her. Without "lower level intellectual ability" children to hold in comparison, she would be nothing.

Adelle's tone conveyed her near-bursting ego. Her words were calculated to ensure that her status would be recognized. She not only felt superior in intellect to her teachers, but she could be heard talking about her parents, particularly her mother, in a patronizing manner. As far as Adelle was concerned, she had few equals. And if she didn't like what a teacher said or taught, she threatened to tell her mother, whom she knew would rush to her defense.

This is a tough situation for a teacher. After all, you're fighting years of parental encouragement and training. You know that this attitude cannot and will not be tolerated in your classroom because it hurts other children and makes them wonder if she is right. Perhaps they *are* inferior in some way. And if that's so, then why try to do better? They will never be as clever as Adelle.

As you can imagine, a child like Adelle can be really, *really* irritating.

It's tempting to want to "teach some manners" to a child like this, and unfortunately, some teachers may resort to humiliation. But humiliation is not a productive answer. It leads to feelings of worthlessness, embarrassment, and loss of confidence. We want to keep Adelle's confidence and self-worth— those are good things; we just want to help her cut the I'm-better-than-you attitude. Besides, we can clearly see from Adelle's behavior that she already *is* insecure. All of her energy is spent in declaring that she has value because she thinks that if she doesn't keep reminding people, they might forget. She's afraid they will.

One way a teacher can help a child like Adelle is through positive reinforcement. Too often we are afraid to give a child like this positive reinforcement because we think it will add to their already overactive ego. Positive reinforcement isn't about appealing to the ego—it's about shoring up a sense of self-worth. Along with positive reinforcement for Adelle's positive behavior, whether it is for her intellectual abilities or other abilities, there will be times when you need to take Adelle aside and ask her how she thinks her bragging and boasting affects her relationships with the other students. There will be opportunities to teach her that each of those other students are good at something, and while they may be different from Adelle, their skills and abilities are just as important. Adelle can learn about persistence from Johnny and about kindness and empathy from Mercedes. You may want to reassure Adelle that you admire her intellectual skills, but that even without those, you would still value her just for herself.

Every child in every class has something of value to offer. Every child deserves recognition for the things she is particularly good at. An intellectually gifted child has a lot to learn from a cheerful child who struggles but doesn't give up. A child with a good work ethic but who doesn't grasp concepts the first time can be a hero to someone else. Don't overlook gifts or have pre-set expectations. There's always something bubbling beneath the surface in each student. Discover what that something is.

Which ability, gift, or talent is the most valuable? It depends on the situation, and it changes as the situation changes. Help all of the children learn to recognize and value the gifts of other children as well as their own gifts. When possible, place the children in learning settings where more than one gift is required to solve a problem.

The idea is not to take away from or devalue who Adelle is or what abilities she has, but to help her recognize the value of the abilities and personalities of others. We heard about a school for gifted children where the gifted students are paired with special education students for part of every day, usually for music or art or a special assembly or speaker. These gifted students not only developed great compassion and tolerance for differences, they also developed friendships with the children who had difficulties. We don't suggest that teachers regularly "use" their brightest students to replace teachers or regularly teach or tutor other students when they could be using the time for their own learning, but it is wonderful when gifted children gain appreciation for the strengths and good qualities in all individuals, as well as empathy for the struggles of others.

Now, let's move on from Adelle for a moment and take a look at another extremely bright, gifted child. This boy, Thad, is an only child, just like Adelle. His parents have always supported him, been involved in his schoolwork, congratulated him on his academic success, and yet never made him feel as though his brainpower were the sole purpose for his continued existence. Thad, who is now in eighth grade, is extremely aware of the feelings of others, and he always has been. He is careful never to say anything that would hurt someone else's feelings, and on the rare occasion that he makes a joke about somebody else, he apologizes immediately—even if they don't appear to be offended. He is conscientious about his schoolwork but doesn't spend much time comparing his abilities to those around him. Thad's biggest challenge is that he's a perfectionist. He compares the work he does with what he thinks he should be able to do. In his mind, he often comes up short, though his parents and teachers would disagree. Thad is humble, but he lacks confidence.

It's a delicate balance. Teachers will have to deal with an endless variety of children who either need to develop their self-worth and confidence or who need to develop a stronger sense of humility. We don't want to go too far in either direction.

One of the best ways to teach students the value of humility is for teachers to emulate that virtue themselves. As teachers, it can be easy to develop a fear that student knowledge of our humility could create a weakness for us. Haven't we all had a student or two who has exploited our weaknesses? The experience is far from enjoyable. To compensate, and to prevent further exploitation, we sometimes tend to cast off our humility and shield ourselves instead with our confidence alone. In some cases, we resort to arrogance and teacher authority—"This is the way it is because I am the teacher, by golly." But what does this teach our students? In particular, if we refuse to acknowledge our shortcomings or that we don't know everything there is to know about a subject, what message are we sending to our gifted students who also feel a pressure to always be confidently at the top of their game? Or right? Or perfect?

One of the biggest issues involved in the overwhelming prospect of educating a roomful of individual brains is humility. Teachers who gain the most respect are usually the ones who are humble. They are the ones who know how much there is to know and how much they don't know. They are comfortable enough with themselves that they don't feel threatened by the idea that their students may sometimes be smarter or wiser than they are or that they might know something they don't. These teachers love and respect the students enough to listen and to be open to other possibilities.

In one second-grade class, the teacher was reading aloud a *Frog and Toad* book that said that Frog and Toad were sitting alone together on a rock. One of the little boys raised his hand and said, "Oh, isn't that an oxymoron—alone and together?"

The teacher said, "You know, I have forgotten what 'oxymoron' means. Would you like to explain it to the class?" Whether or not she knew what it meant, this was a nice way of respecting the child but also reminding him that not everyone knows the word.

It really is okay for a teacher not to know everything. Nobody knows everything. And everyone, even little five-year-olds, often have some bit of knowledge to offer. Gifted teachers are also gifted learners. They know how to look for opportunities to learn from their students. A good learning environment is like good communication—it goes both ways.

Humility can be an important key to unlocking the door of empathy. When a teacher refuses to concern himself over whether or not his authority is being challenged or threatened, his mind is clear to see into the heart and mind of the student. Humility allows a person to see beyond himself, his ego, and his concerns.

Maria clearly excels in many areas—science, writing, reading, debate, history, economics, and more. In fact, she's in the top of the pack in all academic areas, but she also has a firm grasp on humility. Her yearly participation in cross country running provides not only the benefit of exercise and physical fitness, but also the opportunity to strengthen the humble aspects of her multi-faceted personality. Maria is not in the top of the pack in cross country races; she's not even in the middle of the pack. She has consistently placed second or third *to last* in every single race for at least three years. For someone who is used to being a top dog, that sort of showing time after time could be devastating. But not for Maria. She considers her effort-filled—though always lackluster—races to be a way to help her keep a healthy perspective on her talents and abilities. She says it allows her know how the other guy feels—the student who struggles day after day and yet only remains at or near the bottom. For Maria, cross country is pretty much her personal broccoli or brussels sprouts.

Jerome took two semesters of Spanish when he was in middle school and wanted to continue learning the language in high school. But the high school handbook said that there was a prerequisite; students had to take Spanish I before enrolling in Spanish II. The middle school classes were a great beginning exposure to the language, but the high school Spanish I class was taught at a faster pace and in more depth. Jerome wanted to be able to take a fifth year of Spanish while in high school through Independent Study, and in order to fit everything into his four years of high school scheduling, that meant somehow convincing the school to let him skip the first level.

Though it would be a big challenge, and although he wasn't assured in any way of success, he humbly and confidently set his own benchmark. His humility allowed for the possibility of failure; his confidence allowed him to try. Señora Flores gave him additional material to study, and at the end of eighth grade, he took the same first- and second-semester final exams that the high school students took in Spanish I. He passed with flying colors. He had tested out of Spanish I and could enroll in Spanish II as a ninth grader.

In high school, Jerome set himself another benchmark—learning to speak Spanish with a Castilian accent. This could be equated to an American student wanting to learn English with a British accent. The Castilian accent is the one used in Spain, but American schools teach the Latin American accent of Spanish because it is more prevalent in the U.S. Castilian is difficult to master when one doesn't have a model to listen to regularly. Señora Flores didn't speak to the class with a Castilian accent, but she did help Jerome get onto the right track in learning it. And even though his classmates sometimes couldn't understand what he was saying in the language they were all learning, Jerome persisted in learning the Castilian accent. He enjoyed giving himself challenges.

A couple of years later, it all paid off when the class went to Spain for a two-week trip; he was the only one who was fluent enough to blend in with the locals!

Humility allows us to get past our traditional approaches and to see past our own assumptions so that we can understand exactly what each child needs.

When Karen's younger sister Edna was in fourth grade, she had no inclination whatsoever to do her homework. She simply didn't care about it. She didn't care about her grades. She wasn't interested. She had no motivation. Her teacher could have punished her or given her the traditional negative consequences, but Edna didn't care about those either.

The one thing that Edna cared about then—and still cares about today—was her desire to create works of art in almost any medium. In fourth grade, a single piece of colored construction paper was food, drink, and perfume to her, so her teacher ran with that. The teacher looked beyond the usual remedies and instead treated the individual. She didn't just say, "This is just how we do things in my classroom. You will conform." No. She told Edna that for every homework assignment Edna completed and turned in on time, she would get a new piece of construction paper.

You can call it a bribe, but we see it differently. It was a form of negotiation. A matter of respect. The teacher wanted Edna to get an education. She knew that Edna wanted to create. So she told Edna, if you'll work with me here, we can negotiate a little. You cooperate with my wishes; I'll cooperate with yours. They respected each other's needs.

Mrs. Lidstone had a boy in her fourth-grade class who sat at his desk and read, even while she was talking. She allowed him to keep on reading because she could tell that he was catching what he needed to catch from the class. As she spoke to the rest of the class, she would notice that every now and then, he would look up from his book because she was saying something new and interesting that caught his attention. He was able to multi-task, shutting out the stuff he already knew so he could focus on his book, while at the same time keeping an ear open for new information. He always did well on his schoolwork. She placed him in the back of the classroom so that his under-the-desk reading would be less noticeable to the other students. She said that she chose to let him go his own way—because she knew he was capable of doing it. He did well in all of his subjects, so apparently the reading wasn't interfering with his schoolwork.

Interesting! This teacher chose to *allow* this kid to gain a better education. Other teachers might have insisted instead that he put his book away and pay attention. Other teachers might have decided that the goal was to learn *their* way, follow *their* rules, learn material *their* way and at the pace *they* directed. No running ahead. No multi-tasking. No allowances for individuals. Keep everyone in line and on the same page.

See how that lack of humility can sometimes get in the way? When we don't even realize it's happening? We're just going about our business trying to be good teachers. It's easy to fall back on habit or tradition and forget that not all students function best in the classroom environment we provide, despite our good intentions.

Mrs. McGillicuddy stood outside of the principal's office one day and overheard a girl railing on the principal, Mrs. Jones. Mrs. Jones commands great respect, so this was a rather unusual situation. Mrs. McGillicuddy felt tears come to her eyes as she heard all of the abusive things that the girl was saying to Mrs. Jones. But Mrs. Jones knew the girl and knew that much of the anger that the girl was spewing out probably had to do with her difficult family situation. She had enough respect for the girl's feelings that she was able to allow the girl to vent. Mrs. McGillicuddy later asked the principal why she'd allowed the girl to talk to her like that. Mrs. Jones said, "This girl's been struggling with a lot of things. She doesn't know what else to do." Mrs. Jones showed humility and compassion for the student; in that particular case, the girl needed the principal to love her anyway, because it seemed nobody else did.

Students often challenge teachers in more subtle ways. There will be times when the teacher needs to take control of the situation for the sake of the student. But there will be plenty of other times when the best thing a teacher can do is say to the student, "It's okay. You win. I am not your enemy. I am not going to fight you on this."

It's easy to fall into a power-struggle trap, but humility opens minds. It is so easy to categorize children by age, socio-economic level, test scores, and any number of other factors. We sometimes get so caught up in our perceptions that we fail to see a child for who she really is.

One mother began teaching kindergarten in a small, private school when her youngest son Stevie, who was gifted, was almost four years old. She didn't want to leave him at home, so she arranged with the principal that he could come to her class with her. Stevie stayed in her class all year with the five-year-old kindergarteners. He did all of the things they did—until it was time for promotion. In September, Stevie was dismayed to learn that his friends had moved on to first grade and left him still in kindergarten. Naturally, he was upset and wanted to go with them. But he was told, "Sorry. You're not five years old yet. You can't go to first grade."

Well, that made him even more upset. He'd done everything those other kids had done, and he wanted to go to first grade, darn it! So he insisted on standing by the classroom door until they might one day let him in. His mother spoke with the principal about the problem, and the principal said, "All right, just put a chair in the hall in front of the door and let him sit there; he'll get tired of it in a few days." But Stevie didn't give up. After two weeks of sitting in the chair in the hall, the principal said, "Well, let me test him and see what he does know." Sure enough, little Stevie knew everything the other first graders knew, so the principal let him go into the class. An easy decision to accelerate or grade skip.

Lucky for Stevie that his principal was eventually willing to take a good look at the situation, realize that Stevie had different needs and abilities than most of the other children his age, and make an exception to the rule.

Now, let's take a look at children with learning disabilities—something gifted children struggle with as well. How often do we limit them in their curriculum because we have already made certain assumptions about their abilities? What happens when a teacher is humble enough to consider that a student's true potential can never be defined, even with the best of tests?

Mrs. McGillicuddy has had several experiences with special ed. children who were mainstreamed in the classes she worked in, and often it seemed as if all they were doing was sitting in class. But she said that whenever she did a hands-on project, an interesting thing happened. All of a sudden, those resource kids who didn't speak a word all year, at least not an appropriate word, suddenly chirped up and even sometimes chirped brilliance. There was one boy who didn't speak at all in class and was pulled out most of the class time but was allowed to watch a science demonstration that she was presenting. She didn't realize that the demonstration had struck a chord and gotten his gears turning until the next day. When she began asking questions in class, he was the first to raise his hand with the answers, and he answered correctly. Everyone was amazed. No one thought he would even comprehend the subject, let alone take an interest in it. But she said that when she did hands-on lessons where children could hold and touch things, the resource children comprehended it almost as well—and sometimes better—than the other kids in the class. They perked up and became animated. Suddenly, something clicked. It had some meaning to them. It was tangible rather than abstract. They could literally grasp the subject. These children learned when taught in a different modality.

We've come to an "ah-ha" moment. Humility is the forbearer of *flexibility*, and flexibility opens a doorway to an unknown world. When a teacher is flexible, she allows for unexpected, sometimes serendipitous, success. She makes room for incredible stuff that she had no idea was even possible. No matter how optimistic a teacher is, there is no way any teacher can imagine the true potential of a child. It's unfathomable. There's no end to it. And just when you think you've got a finger or a thumb on it, and sometimes if you try to channel it, the kid yawns, eyeballs the clock, and counts to 60 over and over in an attempt to make the minutes go away.

Flexibility paved the way for Jerome to test out of Spanish I, Mrs. McGillicuddy's second and third graders to learn advanced material in entomology, Mrs. Carmichael's students to take on the trial of Goldilocks and the Three Bears, Maria to experiment with a myriad unusual science projects, and Charlie to teach his instructor another way to correctly complete a math problem. Flexibility is also the tool we need when dealing with asynchronous children—we need to meet their needs on a variety of levels, whether it's providing an accelerated curriculum or an appropriate peer group.

And humble old humility makes all of that flexibility possible. We've known principals to be flexible, too.

A teacher asked one of our principals about the location of a missing student. "Oh," he said, "he's in my office. He's sitting under my desk with headphones, listening to classical music."

This kid needed some space. The principal knew him well enough to give him what he needed, and he had enough of an open mind to allow that child to handle his difficulties himself in the way that best suited him. He didn't hand him a cupcake and try to become his buddy, and he didn't just hand him an after-school detention slip. He would not necessarily treat another student the same way because the next student would have his own set of needs—different needs.

Humility also allows us to go on smiling when things go awry because we are able to take things less personally. Those students sitting in the desks facing you don't always make life easy. Kids can be as stubborn as adults. They don't like to be told what to do all of the time. They don't always want to cooperate. It's like those fantasy conversations that you have in your head when you need to confront someone and you have the whole string of events mentally planned ahead of time. She's going to say that, and I'm going to say this. Then, she'll get upset and say such-and-such, and I'll zing her with my really cool come-back, after which she'll be devastated, humble, apologetic, and she'll worship my brilliant and all-wise mind.

Okay, by a show of hands—how many of you have ever had an imagined conversation go exactly as planned when carried out? No one? Why? Because the other person has a mind of her own. It stinks, we know. But what can you do?

Well, a little humility might help you at least make it through the day. Sometimes, when you are working with young, innocent, and very honest children, you don't have much choice.

When Mrs. McGillicuddy was working with different groups of kids, she would usually go into the classrooms to get them. On a normal day, as if she ever had a normal day in her life, she wore her hair straight. But one day she was feeling a little in need of a vanity boost, and she decided to curl it. She thought it looked pretty good. She walked into the first-grade room to get her group, and as she walked in, half of the kids in the class looked at her and said, "Mrs. McGillicuddy, what did you do to your hair? Do you have bedhead?"

Sometimes humility is forced upon us.

Another day, after she had colored her hair, mostly to get rid of the skunk stripe along her hair part, she walked into the same classroom and the kids asked, "Mrs. McGillicuddy! Do you have a wig on?"

Leave it to those honest, ego-deflating children to keep the rest of us in line just when we think we're looking pretty good.

Once, when Mrs. Chrisman was discussing with her class the value and purpose of eyelashes, she mentioned that Eskimos and football players darken the areas around their eyes to eliminate the reflections of the sun in their eyes. One of her students raised his hand and told her, "Your mascara is smudged above your left eye."

She said, "Thanks for pointing that out. I hadn't noticed."

Then he said, "Oh, it's always like that."

Whether they're pointing out your cosmetic defects or the shortcomings of your presentation on the origins of early civilization, kids are observant—that's a good thing. Let them be honest. Okay, perhaps a little lesson in tact would be in order now and then, but allow them to express their feelings. Don't place yourself on a pedestal, surround yourself with students, and expect that none of them will take a chip out every now and then—maybe even a huge chunk. Get right down there on the solid ground with them and take their constructive criticism when they really do have a point. If a kid says, "This is boring!" then perhaps you could ask him to rephrase that in a more constructive and helpful way and ask him to offer some solutions to the problem. If they are good solutions, take them. If not, come up with some ideas of your own and make some changes. Because if a kid says the lesson is boring, it's probably because it's boring.

This is where humility comes in again. Gifted teachers value what their students have to offer them, even when it's uncomfortable.

Any good leader can value what his opponents have to offer, even though it might be hard to swallow. When making selections for his Cabinet, did Lincoln choose his campaign allies? Nope. He chose people for his Cabinet who were his major *rivals* for the Republican party's Presidential nomination. It takes humility to appreciate the talents of your rivals! But as with Lincoln, it can also be good political move.

Let's face it—there is yet to be found a perfect educator. The old "to err is human" thing keeps getting in the way.

Teachers are not perfect people, and while this can help to keep them humble, it is good for the rest of us to remember, too. They are not gods. They are, every now and then, going to leak their humanity in a way so obvious that even the students in the back row can't deny it. And their modeling of this difficult-to-attain trait can then help the students find ways to reach it themselves.

12: Honoring the Child

"Life is not easy for any of us. But what of that?
We must have perseverance and above all confidence in ourselves.
We must believe that we are gifted for something
and that this thing must be attained."
~ Marie Curie ~

Any teacher can understand the meanings and nuances to the phrase "sometimes you just have to go with the flow." And when there's a gifted child in your classroom, sometimes that flow can easily pull the rug out from under you.

Here, Tamara relays for us an example of one gifted child taking the reins, and the wonderful lessons that can be learned when that happens:

All teachers know that flexibility is important. I've learned that when it comes to teaching gifted kids, flexibility is imperative.

My sixth-grade GT students meet with me on an alternating schedule, one group one day, and the other group the next day. Since our school colors are purple and gold, all sixth graders in my class are in one or the other—Purple or Gold—so those teams define my sixth-grade groups.

When my students reach sixth grade, I find that they are more in need of class discussions during that year than during the other years of their school careers. Not that we don't have important and necessary discussions during other years, but the unique combination of traits in sixth-grade gifted students— energy level, hormones kicking in, other students noticing and commenting on the differences and quirks of my gifted students, changing teachers for the first time, etc.—requires paying attention to emotional needs—and thus, Vent Time.

My Gold group one year consisted of 13 energetic and talkative 12-year-old souls. Well, a few of them weren't very talkative, but the rest of the crew made up for the ones who were quiet. Here are brief descriptions of the dozen plus one.

Earl has a finely-tuned sense of humor and never fails to find the tiniest of opportunities to be funny. He also competes in calf roping. I've seen him in action and am impressed with how quick, gentle, accurate, bold, and honest he is in competition.

Bjorn is a budding ornithologist who raises emus and other exotic birds. His list of chores for taking care of his birds would curl the toes on most kids, but for this young man of 12, the birds are his lifelong passion. Bjorn is entirely comfortable being his own unique self, and he helps to inspire the others in the class to be so as well.

Sara is defined by curiosity. She asks questions about everything and persists until she reaches a satisfactory level of understanding. Fairly quiet in her other classes, she bursts from the seams in my room with comments, questions, and ideas.

Adelina approaches challenges with the quiet, determined calm so common to her tribal culture. She is not boisterous like most middle graders, which would lead many to think that she is shy or unmotivated, but in reality, she is persistent, hardworking, and steadfast in the face of any odds. And she has certainly already overcome some steep odds.

Atsuko learns with matter-of-fact ease and aspires to one day be a paleontologist. She approaches everything in life with deep thoughtfulness, and everyone knows when she speaks up in class that she has already analyzed every angle of what she is about to say.

Lew barely talks in my class, which is more than he talks in any of his regular classes. He's not painfully shy, just unusually quiet. He is a deep, deep sponge who absorbs more from the world around him than most people are even aware is there. He's also an underachieving gifted student. His grades don't even come close to reflecting his ability level or intelligence. Like many middle school gifted students, he lets his grades slip to hide just a bit.

Ford is part of the reason my lesson plan went out the window one memorable day. Ford joined up with us at the beginning of fifth grade, whereas I had been working with most of the other students since they were in kindergarten. Prior to that, Ford bounced in and out of a couple of different schools, and fourth grade saw him sitting in the hallway blowing off steam most days. Behavior problems were a part of almost every day for him. Thankfully, his fourth-grade teachers were able to see through the filter of his rough exterior to the intelligence and ability inside him. He was such a complex boy that it took an entire year of filtering, but by the end of the year, we knew he should join the gifted class. The first few times he came with us in fifth grade, he actually sat under the table. In his mind, he couldn't imagine that he belonged in this classroom for bright students. He didn't see himself as even average, let alone smart. Bless their souls, the other kids in the group were the perfect balance of understanding and encouragement, and they weren't the least bit pushy. They gave him room but also let him know that he was a welcome part of the group. We held class on the floor for a few weeks to adapt to his comfort zone of the space under the table. By the third week, he came out from under the table and joined us on the floor. Though he still struggles with some self-doubts, Ford has made steady progress since then, particularly in terms of his behavior and academic attitude.

Jarrett is two years ahead in math and could beat his dad at chess by age four. He has been quiet since kindergarten but always shines in whatever fashion he chooses. His insight never ceases to amaze me.

Jill…. Jill is the other reason my lesson plans went out the window that day. She is the prime culprit, in fact. Jill moved to our district in second grade, not long after the tragic death of her mother. For the first three or four years that I worked with her, she was shy, quiet, and reserved, but sixth grade saw an incredible awakening. She would literally bounce or dance into class some days. Her vocabulary is so keen that the other students in the group often tease her good-naturedly about being a walking dictionary. From them, she takes it well, and she encourages them to look up the words she uses that they don't know. She is a lightbulb of spunk.

Michelle is true grit. The physical and psychological strength in her thin body is quite impressive. The oldest of four, she is often responsible for the younger ones, who are each a handful on their own. Michelle was born to run, and she holds our school's record for her mile time. She has competed in the Junior Olympics, and after school as I walk back to the middle school from the high school, I often see her racing down the sidewalk trying to outrun the school busses.

Kay is pure kindness and approaches her schoolwork, friends, family, peers, and life with a deep reverence that reflects a level of maturity few adults ever reach. Highly sensitive, she sees and feels aspects of relationships that give them more meaning for her.

Cree grew about a foot between the fifth and sixth grades, and I imagine he will soon outgrow all of the teachers in the school. Cree is one of those gifted kids whose brain is going in so many different directions all at once that he exhibits some ADHD-type behaviors. In his case, it's not ADHD, but he's a good example of why some gifted children are misdiagnosed as ADHD. Cree is interested in just about everything, will debate just about everything, and actually knows something about just about everything. Knowledge is energy for Cree.

Haiden loves to make others laugh and hopes to someday do so through the world of acting. His somewhat oversized frame leads to teasing from his peers, which he deflects with some of his funniest jokes. Though his size and jovial nature imply otherwise, Haiden is actually one of the most sensitive students in the group.

Quite a combination, these 13, aren't they? Because our district is on an Indian Reservation, the ethnicity in this class, as in all of my classes, is mixed. The proportion of Native American and non-Native students that I work with is equivalent to the proportion of Native and non-Native students in our district's total student population. But regardless of ethnicity, the diverse personality traits probably reflect the many variations found in gifted children everywhere.

An advantage of working with the same students for multiple consecutive years is that, just as I get to know them better, they also get to know each other better, and they become a cohesive support network for one another as a result. This class in particular had a true family or team feel to it, and they had become keenly aware of each other's strengths, weaknesses, and struggles over the years.

On the day my lesson plan flew out the window, I had the tables pushed back to open up space in the middle of my small classroom for a circle of 14 chairs. I always sit facing the clock because if I don't, we all lose track of time and forget to wrap the discussion up before the bell rings. I was prepared that day with a topic (multipotentiality) and a list of questions.

An increasing amount is being said, written, and researched about the social and emotional needs of gifted students. Those of us who work full-time with these fascinating creatures are well aware of the unique issues and struggles that find their way into the lives of gifted children. Perfectionism, dealing with high expectations from themselves and others, underachievement, multipotentiality, and heightened sensitivities are just a few examples. I've found over the years that if I have specific discussions with my gifted students about these and other topics, they develop a better understanding of themselves in the process, along with strategies for dealing with these issues. Seeing them become emotionally healthier is all the motivation I need.

Multipotentiality, literally, is the state of having multiple potentials. While everyone in the world has something they're good at, gifted kids generally have many somethings they're good at. And although there are lots of nice features to multi-potentiality, it comes with some challenges, too. Because they have many passionate interests, for example, it's common for gifted students to struggle mightily when choosing a college major. Secondly, excelling in so many areas can find them overbooked with commitments involving all of their various talents. Yet because they love each one so much, they prefer to precipitously juggle all of the options rather than taking what some would call the realistic option and just cut one or two out for now. As a GT specialist, it is part of my job to help them decide what the right balance is between juggling and cutting—and how to make their own decisions about when to do each.

Very early on in the discussion that day, Jill hopped out of her chair and proclaimed a tangent to our topic: "What we need here, folks, is an Honoring."

"A what?"

"An Honoring."

Ford was struggling a bit in our discussion because he had yet to let himself acknowledge that he had more than a single talent.

Jill took a small step toward him and said, "Ford, I honor you because I think you're really smart and I know you don't think you are, but believe me, you are. And I admire how much you've changed for the better these past couple of years. You used to, well, you used to pop your cork pretty often, and you don't anymore, and I'm proud of you for turning yourself around. I honor you for letting us help you see what was inside of you all along."

Ford turned a bit red in dumbfounded discomfort and looked nervously at his shoes. But I noticed a small smile on his face. He doesn't smile very often.

We all sat there in shock as Jill took over. She'd become spunkier that year, and now we were all caught off guard by just how much so. She kept right on going without missing a beat.

"Lew, I honor you because you notice things that no one else does. You may not talk much, but I think that's just because you have so much to think about."

"Michelle, I honor you because, wow, because you are just the neatest person ever, and I'm so glad we've become friends and you support me and listen, and man, can you ever run! I can see the spirits of your proud ancestors in the wind behind you as you race. I'm going to cheer you on in the Olympics someday!"

As teachers, we all know that sometimes you just have to go with the flow. I can't be a control freak teaching gifted kids. Sometimes I have to throw caution to the wind and see what happens. If I had reined her in and refocused the group on our discussion topic, we all would've missed out on what turned out to be one of the most memorable and important days in our class and in our lives. They would've let me rein her in, and she would've let me, too. She knew she was stepping on my plans.

But I let her go.

She proceeded around the circle, student to student, honoring each one of them in a public yet gentle and very accurate way. With insights far beyond her years but entirely reflective of her intelligence and sensitivity, she honored everyone in the room, myself included, and left us with a short moment of hushed awe.

Then Haiden stood up and gently set Jill back in her chair and said, "Jill, I—no, we—we honor you because you teach us new words and you, wow, I don't even know if there are words to describe how incredible you are, and you inspire me, and all of us, to do better and be better. Plus, you're the only person who will do the Happy Dance with me." The Happy Dance was a silly little jig that one or the both of them had made up. They did it in tandem some days after class because it cheered them up and made everyone else grin.

Haiden then continued around the room, honoring each of his classmates with his own insights about their strengths and unique qualities. And before Haiden was even done, Michelle was already out of her seat and waiting her turn.

They all did it, and I followed suit as well. We all still refer to that day as The Honoring Day. Jill came up to me after class to apologize for sweeping away my plans, but I told her that I was thankful for her and for her idea and that she had turned the class into an opportunity none of us would forget.

Classrooms *are* places of honoring. Every teacher has her own way of highlighting the uniqueness and specialness of each child. As well, it's okay to acknowledge that those quirky gifted kids have a degree of uniqueness that varies even more than that of the average bear. They *do* stand out. It is only when we know the ways in which they are different that we can begin to understand them. And it is when we understand them that we will be best able to meet their intellectual and social/emotional needs. With those needs met, they will then be better able to, as Marie Curie put it, attain what they are gifted for.

We'd like to end with one last quote. It's from an Apple Computer® advertisement:

> *Here's to the crazy ones.*
> *The misfits.*
> *The rebels.*
> *The troublemakers.*
> *The round pegs in the square holes.*
> *The ones who see things differently.*
> *They're not fond of rules.*
> *And they have no respect for the status quo.*

You can praise them, disagree with them, quote them,
      disbelieve them, glorify or vilify them.
About the only thing that you can't do is ignore them.
Because they change things.
They invent. They imagine. They heal.
They explore. They create. They inspire.
They push the human race forward.
Maybe they have to be crazy.
How else can you stare at an empty canvas and see a work of art?
Or sit in silence and hear a song that's never been written?
Or gaze at a red planet and see a laboratory on wheels?
We make tools for these kinds of people.
While some may see them as the crazy ones, we see genius.
Because the ones who are crazy enough to think that they
      can change the world are the ones who do.[19]

And you, oh readers, you are the brain motivators, the creativity inspirers, and the seed planters. You are the oil in the gears, and the bearers of light.

You are the teachers. You are the gifted teachers.

13: In Their Own Voices

"Getting things right is the strategy that my teacher says I should work with. I think that's pretty boring. Don't you?"
~ Gregory, age eight, third grade ~

Tamara learned that one of the most important things to consider when teaching gifted kids is to create for them a place where they can safely be, well, themselves. These kids are quirky, different, out-of-the-box, and unique in countless ways. Fun for some of them is reading the encyclopedia, or dissecting a dead cockroach, or seeing who can solve a difficult math problem the quickest. Our world *needs* people like this, yet their peer culture (and frankly, our whole society's culture) often puts them down for being smart and curious and a bit strange or "weird." This is one of the biggest tragedies of our time. Anyone who thinks gifted children, just by being gifted, have everything going for them should take some time to talk with a group of gifted kids about their thoughts, feelings, and opinions and find out what the world is *really* like for them.

Tamara makes it a point to do this a couple of times a week with her students. Most poignantly, one of them once said to her, "Miss Fisher, your classroom is the only place where I feel like I can truly be myself."

On one hand, how sad that this child's life is devoid of other places where she feels she can be herself. On the other hand, at least there is one place where she can.

Here, some gifted students tell what they like about their GT class:

"I have less stress because I'm learning more." (first grader)
"Now I know I'm not alone." (fourth grader)
"It's a lot harder, and when it's really hard, my head starts to hurt. I think it's fun." (fourth grader)
Just KNOWING that there is a place where intelligence and ability are stretched and appreciated, rather than seen as an inconvenience, is enough to keep me going." (eleventh grader)

Gifted students need some place to go, some community that they can identify with, some authority figure who can understand them and guide them along the way. It's like the theme song to *Cheers*—you know, everybody knows your name, they're always glad you came, blah blah blah—except that Carla the waitress might not be the best candidate to be a GT teacher.

The most important thing, though, is that gifted kids be accepted and understood. The trait-themed chapters of this book have aimed to do just that. For deeper insights, we will now take a look at what may be going on inside the brain of the average (as if!) GT student.

It's not easy to find out what they're thinking. For example, let's imagine you are a second-grade teacher and that you have a very quiet and well-behaved student sitting at the front of your class. Let's say that this student's name is Karen. Karen sits there and follows along with the science textbook, sort of, as each of the students in the class reads out loud about Sir Isaac Newton and his discovery of gravity. Karen gets good grades, demonstrates comprehension skills, and never causes any trouble for anyone. Her only really obvious flaw is that sometimes she shows up for school with her dress on inside out. As you momentarily stop the oral read-along and discuss the subject for a moment, you notice that Karen is making eye contact with you and seems to be aware that there is an important scientific conversation occurring which is deserving of her attention.

Okay, here goes: Is she thinking, "Wow! Science is so fascinating, and Isaac Newton was an important player in the study of gravitational pull, and how cool is that? No wonder he's in the textbooks!"?

No. No matter how complacent she appears on the surface, no matter how she seems to be soaking up the information like a good little second-grade sponge, this is what she is *really* thinking: "This is devastating! Here's a guy who sat under a tree and had the misfortune of having an apple fall on his head. That was *it*? *That's* how he discovered gravity? Whoop-de-doo! He couldn't have been all that smart. It's not as if he could have been the first person to notice that when things fall, they fall downward. Were people so clueless before that? Dang, *I* could have discovered gravity—and I could have been famous for it!"

Karen decides then and there that all of the easy discoveries are probably already taken. She also holds Sir Isaac Newton in very low esteem.

But as her teacher, you would never know from looking at her.

As you scan the eyes of your students for signs of intelligent life, how do you know which kids are actually engaged in the current topic and which kids are bored out of their minds, frustrated, off thinking about other planets, or miserable yet docile? How do you reach them? How do you get into the heads of your gifted students so you can better understand what's happening in there and better help them to make the most of their educational opportunities?

We've found one scientific method of discovery to be invaluable. It works. Just ask, "Hey, what's going on in there?" Go ahead. Don't be afraid. The truth shall set you free. It might make you cringe a little, but a little cringing never hurt anybody, did it?

So we've stepped out on a ledge, prepared our cringing facial expressions, and asked gifted children from across the country a few important questions about their educations. Here, in their own voices, are thoughts from gifted kids from first grade right on up through college. Some answers will surprise you; others will not. Many answers will have a lot in common with each other, while others are contradictory. That goes to show that while it's important to understand the characteristics of gifted children in general, they are always also individuals.

Elementary Students

What are the advantages of being smart?

- You can invent.

- Being able to do things that I never knew before.

- You get done first and you get more time to read.

- Work is easy.

- We get to go to GT and do hard, fun stuff.

- Being able to work ahead.

- The advantages of being smart are you can get a scholarship to college and you can get a good job with lots and lots of money.

- People admire me.

What are the disadvantages of being smart?

- One of the bad things about being smart is sometimes you get all mixed up in your head and it turns into a big mess.

- You might go fast and write the wrong answer.

- We end up running out of work.

- Sometimes when we go to GT, we have to stay in from recess to catch up on regular work.

- You never really get to do anything in school because you're sort of ahead of everyone else.

- The disadvantages of being smart are that you get called a geek, and there are people who are smart that have been called crazy.

- Sometimes you get stuff so easy that when something hard comes along, it is tough because you are not used to it.

How would you define "smart"?

- I think it means to think creatively.

- Smart means you have a thinking advantage.

- I would define "smart" as people who have known how to read, do math, have known history, and have known how to survive in the wilderness with only half a sandwich since they were six years old.

What style of teacher do you most like to learn from and why? (characteristics)

- The style of teacher I like to learn from is a teacher who stretches your abilities.

- I like the kind of teachers who are challenging, and I like teachers who if you ask a question they can answer it and they give you comments on papers.

- I like to learn from a teacher that is nice and kind and doesn't yell in an angry voice because I get scared of very loud angry voices.

What style of teacher do you least like to learn from and why? (characteristics)

- I don't like teachers with low expectations.

- She has too many rules.

- Non-interactive.
- A very mean teacher because mean teachers will most likely kill you if you don't spell "hypothesis."
- I don't like teachers that read without expression and who don't really challenge you or don't really laugh a lot, and who don't really do a lot of challenges or don't reward you.

What do you wish your teachers knew or understood about you?

- I wish I could think of a better way to say this, but every single paper is too easy and it's a waste of time for me.
- I wish they wouldn't use me like a last resort of someone to call on.
- I wish my teachers knew that sometimes I feel like I'm only learning things I already know.
- I wish my teachers understood that I have a good brain and I want to use it for school.

What do you wish other kids knew or understood about you?

- I am not a nerd!
- I wish that kids understood that I need challenge.
- I wish that people would understand that we just learn differently.

What kinds of strategies have your teachers used over the years that help to create a positive learning environment for students like you?

- They've taught me to keep stickin' to it.
- They let me look for different ways to solve other problems.
- They let me go to GT.

- We use lots of learning games.

- They make me laugh.

- A strategy my teachers have used to create a positive learning environment is not cussing.

What do you think teachers need to know about gifted students?

- They need to remember that we want to learn, too.

- I know this sounds mean, but I really don't like to be with kids at a lower level.

- They need to know that we get bored.

- WE NEED *HARDER WORK!!!!!*

- To focus on all of us. She only focuses on the struggling kids.

- I wish that they would know if we already learned it.

- Sometimes we get frustrated.

- We need to exercise our gifts more often.

If you could change something about school, what would it be and why?

- It would be that the teachers would let you finish your sentence.

- I wish we could learn about everything we want.

- I would have students teaching teachers because they need to learn some things.

What would school be like for you if there were no gifted and talented program or class? Why?

- It would be so boring. You wouldn't get as much peace and quiet. It just makes your brain build up with ideas!

🔢 Oh, it would be very bad! I probably would shrink back to a lower level.

🔢 I would go somewhere where there was GT.

🔢 My brain would start to hurt because I would not be able to use it.

🔢 That would be a BAD DEAL because my brain would break down without GT class. And for another thing I would cry.

🔢 It would be hard on me to not have GT, but then again, school would be easy.

Middle-Grade Students

What are the advantages of being smart?

🔢 An advantage of being smart is that sometimes my brain calculates answers before I think about them.

🔢 I think the advantages of being smart are that you usually get better grades and you are complimented on stuff you got right.

🔢 I can help all my friends with their homework if they need help. And it gives you a good feeling to be able to do that—to help someone raise their grades.

What are the disadvantages of being smart?

🔢 I don't like it when people try to cheat off my papers or get mad at me when I won't give them an answer.

🔢 The disadvantages of being smart are being chosen because you are smart, not because you are a good friend. Everyone relies on you to get the right answer.

🔢 Always having to be the "teacher" for other students.

⊞ People may make fun of you. It might be harder to make friends.

⊞ Other people don't understand you. They might think you're stuck up or a know-it-all.

⊞ When everyone wants help, you don't have enough time to do what you want to do.

How would you define "smart"?

⊞ Smart is knowing more than the teacher teaches you.

⊞ You don't have to be taught over and over.

What style of teacher do you most like to learn from and why? (characteristics)

⊞ If I ask a lot of questions, they don't get frustrated.

⊞ I like learning from a teacher who *really* understands me and who knows my abilities.

⊞ A teacher who is creative and makes lessons INTERESTING.

⊞ I like to learn things from teachers who relate themselves to students. Then you can listen and absorb more things from them than teachers who place themselves on a throne.

What style of teacher do you least like to learn from and why? (characteristics)

⊞ Teachers who ignore kids they don't like.

⊞ I don't like to learn from teachers that want stuff to be done their way, the "my way or the highway" option.

What do you wish your teachers knew or understood about you?

- Even though I skipped a grade, I do not feel smarter than everyone else.

- I don't like to look at teachers but I do listen to what they say.

- Just because I'm smart doesn't mean that I'm going to get straight A's. I STILL MAKE MISTAKES!

What do you wish other kids knew or understood about you?

- I *like* being different.

- Something I wish kids knew about me is even though in some cases I'm more academically advanced, I'm going through the same things they are.

- I'm not perfect. Whenever I get something wrong, they act like I should know everything and get it right.

- They don't always have to come to me for help.

What kinds of strategies have your teachers used over the years that help to create a positive learning environment for students like you?

- Some of my teachers have had me do harder versions of the assignments.

- Well, that thing called the Principal's Office....

- They make challenges, like if we were doing a one-step equation, then for us they would make a two-step equation.

What do you think teachers need to know about gifted students?

- We can lose our homework sometimes.

- WE DON'T KNOW EVERYTHING.

- I think that teachers need to know that we're not gifted in everything. We may excel in some subjects, while in others we are not as great.

- We're just kids.

- We learn differently than normal students.

If you could change something about school, what would it be and why?

- I would change the way that gifted kids get treated so they are challenged more.

- The assignments are stupid, asking us the same bloody questions over and over, making us so bored with them that we will speed through them and then miss the easy problems.

What would school be like for you if there were no gifted and talented program or class? Why?

- We wouldn't get to hang out with kids at the same academic level during school time.

- It would be horrible! For eight years of my life I've been in GT. You grow in it. I guess you could go so far as to say you get addicted to it. You get really annoyed easily without it. This challenging learning environment really allows you to open up and share your feelings with a feeling of safety.

- It would be different. I probably would still be in eighth-grade math if there wasn't a GT program. But now I'm in tenth-grade math, two years ahead.

High School and College Students

What are the advantages of being smart?

▦ Everything. Well, not really. It's easier to be depressed when you are a philosopher.

▦ It is not so much about being smart but about having a spark inside that can be coaxed to flame.

▦ I am able to carry on intellectual conversations with people much older than me. I feel more confident about school than most people do.

▦ Being smart broadens your perspectives because you are able to understand many things from various areas; it encourages learning of those things you don't know.

▦ The main advantage of being smart, for me, was not having to work as hard at learning concepts or memorizing information as most of my classmates, which freed me up to work more creatively and independently. I think I was able to do more, in terms of enrichment activities like special-interest classes, independent projects, and extra-curricular activities.

What are the disadvantages of being smart?

▦ There are a few disadvantages of being smart. You are bored a lot in class and you become restless very easily.

▦ A disadvantage of being smart is that I am constantly put into the "smart" group and always expected to fit everyone else's expectations of that group. I, in turn, become way too hard on myself.

▦ I just imagine how wonderful it would be to go to school and feel totally stretched—pushed to my limits and past.

Instead, it is my responsibility to push myself and map out the edges of what I can do.

- Being smart puts you on a different level of expectation. You're expected to be at the top of your class, pass every test, and succeed at everything you do.

- Teachers usually keep to their own agendas and just forget about the smart kids.

- I think a lot of cynical thoughts sometimes and then wonder if I would be happier if I weren't as intelligent. On top of all that, I feel separated from everyone else in my age group. It's very hard for me to relate to people.

- There will always be those who refuse to understand motivation and its purpose in my eyes, and who will either do their very most to bring me down or clutch onto me for a free ride to the top.

How would you define "smart"?

- If you are academically smart, then you do well in school, but if you are emotionally smart, then you may not be very good at math or any other subject, but you can tell how people are feeling and can figure out what you can do to help them.

- Smart is being smart enough to know you don't know everything but stupid enough to want to.

- I believe "smart" is a term often used to describe the ability to regurgitate answers, which is not always as negative as it sounds. However, intelligence is the ability to deduce one's own conclusions. I would much rather be intelligent.

- I would define "smart" as a natural passion to gain knowledge and, more importantly, the necessary persistence and patience embedded with that passion.

What style of teacher do you most like to learn from and why? (characteristics)

⊞ I like a teacher who gives me a goal that I think will be impossible to reach, but by the end of the year I have achieved it. I like this because it shows me that I have made visible progress.

⊞ I like teachers who have a new project or challenge ready for me when I finish another. I like teachers that are constantly asking the class thought-provoking questions.

⊞ I like to learn from teachers whose emphasis is learning, not difficulty, because it's not relevant for a class to be really difficult. Learning matters more.

⊞ I am more influenced by teachers who show that they love what they do. When it is apparent that they love what they do, that energy is intoxicating, and it makes me want to learn why, and it makes me interested in what they do.

⊞ Professors and teachers I enjoy the most are those who structure their classes with independent discovery projects, with available support for questions.

⊞ I like to learn from a teacher who can guide me from theory to applicability. I appreciate knowing why it's important for me to learn something and how I can use it. However, I don't like being condescended to.

What style of teacher do you least like to learn from and why? (characteristics)

⊞ I don't appreciate teachers who only accept or look for correct answers, or go straight from the textbooks. I think teachers who do those things could loosen up a little and still stay on task.

- I hate having to be taught by teachers who make you follow the pace of the slowest student.

- The style of teaching that is my least favorite is the type that does nothing but lecture the class on their ideas but are unwilling to hear ours or question various beliefs.

- I'm never comfortable learning from people who make themselves superior to their students, who don't care about what they teach, or who don't take charge.

- I find it hard to learn from teachers who simply tell you to open a book, read a chapter, do "book work," and give us a test over that chapter.

- Teachers who don't update lesson plans to fit the real world.

What do you wish your teachers knew or understood about you?

- I wish that my teachers understood that I am usually only serious in class, and that isn't how my whole life is. I wish they understood that I am not too concerned with my grade. I have had teachers tell me to lighten up about my grade. Usually the only reason that I have given them to say such a thing is that I occasionally ask to see if I am missing anything. In my opinion, this is one of the worst things they could tell me. Sometimes it seems that teachers think that just because I come up to them and tell them that they have graded one of my papers wrong instead of just leaving it, they automatically think that all I care about is my grade. This is not true.

- I wish that my teachers understood that I care about my grade, more so than they do, and thus a forgotten homework assignment or a poor grade is not a personal affront to them, but an accident.

- I would like my teachers to know that I like to figure stuff out for myself and that they don't need to give us homework on simple things that don't test my knowledge.

- I wish my teachers knew I didn't need things beaten into my head 50 times to get me to remember something.

- I wish my teachers realized how much I care about learning and that they need to let the people who want to learn, learn!

- I wish my teachers understood that I have many things going on and I get overloaded and stressed out. I wish they would be more lenient on due dates. Sometimes there's just too much all at one time.

- I wish they could tell when I'd been up all night reading Jane Eyre and that it shook me to the bedrock and understand that was why my homework was a little lackluster. I wish they could see that the book was more important. I wish they could see that I hadn't spent my night watching television and avoiding work, I'd spent it renovating myself. I wish they could see that I want them to make their _class_ what keeps me up at night. I wish they would.

- I wish my teachers understood that I am ambitious! I just have appalling time management skills.

- I wish my teachers understood that I work best on my own; if I need help, I ask for it. I don't like group work or someone breathing down my neck.

What do you wish other kids knew or understood about you?

- I wish other kids knew that I don't try to be an "overachiever" and that I am just a normal student trying to do well in school.

▦ I would like for my "peers" to understand that my failures in social interactions do not translate into me giving them the cold shoulder.

▦ I wish that other students would understand that I do not like it when they try to compare themselves to me. I think everyone has their own characteristics.

▦ I wish other kids understood that the reason I am so diligent in my studies is because it is a way for me to challenge myself. I challenge myself to get my work done quickly and nicely. Kids always wonder why I do so much homework and take so many classes. It's my only way to enjoy school.

What kinds of strategies have your teachers used over the years that help to create a positive learning environment for students like you?

▦ I have had teachers who have given the class an assignment that is open-ended, and so for those of us that may need a challenge, we can do as much work as we want, instead of some classes where we may just fill in the answer to a question.

▦ They use things that we like to do to show us what they want us to know.

▦ The most "positive learning environments" I have been subject to are classes in which I am most independent, am allowed space to think, and am given back my freedom of expression.

▦ The times that I have had a positive learning experience are when teachers acknowledge me and go the extra step to challenge me. I get really bored, and once I'm bored, I just shut off and have a bad attitude.

What do you think teachers need to know about gifted students?

- I think that teachers need to know that we have a different line of thought and that we need more of different things and less of the same old, same old.

- I think that some teachers need to understand that there is such a thing as a gifted student. All students are not created equal. Forcing a gifted student to repeat a topic which they have already learned not only doesn't teach them anything, it can cause them to lose interest, sometimes resulting in a serious drop in grades.

- I think teachers need to know that when we are bored, it's not that we are being rude or disinterested, it's just that we aren't learning anything new, and as a result, we feel we are wasting our time.

- Teachers need to know that we don't view ourselves as superior to our peers in any way; it's just that we want to be challenged a bit more.

- I think that teachers need to know that gifted students have the ability to take their knowledge to the next level and may need help to do so.

- I think many gifted students are passionate about certain things and if teachers encouraged these areas, it would be beneficial for the growth of gifted students.

If you could change something about school, what would it be and why?

- If I could change anything about school, it would be to create more advanced classes and to sort them so they are available all throughout the day, not crammed into the last two class periods. That way, students who choose to excel are not forced to choose between the four advanced classes they want.

▦ I would change how strict the classes are. I don't like being punished for other people's actions, and you learn much better if you like the atmosphere.

▦ If I could change something about school, it would be that the "advanced" classes weren't just seen as something to put on a resume, but rather as an actual advanced class where we were free of the kids who just do enough work to get the grade but don't really care.

▦ I would make classes based on intelligence. This was more relevant when I was younger because now I can take AP classes, and the GT class, and Honors classes. When I was little I was often bored to tears in classes going over times tables for the third time…again, when I got it last week. If one or two students don't understand it, *they* just do it again. Also, students should be rewarded for going beyond, not for doing what they are SUPPOSED to do. For example, some kids at my other school were given candy for doing their homework. I did my homework but was not given candy. These kids get it in their head that mediocrity is okay as long as you do what you are supposed to do.

▦ If I could change something about school, it would be the amount of time that is wasted. I think there are such better ways to use time, but as students, we have to stay at school and waste large parts of our day.

▦ I would want to have more AP and alternative subject classes so that smarter students can learn more and learn new things not typically taught in high school.

▦ I wish my teachers weren't under such pressure to make everyone feel good about themselves through grade inflation, because university professors aren't. I wish my teachers had higher standards for all of us and a magic wand to motivate the less-motivated so classes wouldn't be such a drag.

What would school be like for you if there were no gifted and talented program or class? Why?

▦ I think school would be pretty boring because I wouldn't have a class to look forward to. I feel more comfortable and relaxed in GT because I know that I don't have to have any specific person's ideas being woven into my work. Everything that I do in here can be unique and original.

▦ There would be far more work and less real *learning*.

▦ I think that perhaps I wouldn't have found my interest in photography until much later. Because I got to choose a photography-based project [in GT class], I was able to find what motivates me early on. I was better prepared then to decide what I wanted to do in the future.

▦ I would have been more confused about myself. The GT program helped me understand that there are more people out there who are like me, and that it isn't a bad thing.

There you have it—straight from the mouths of gifted students. No middleman to twist or tame their words. It is fascinating not only to hear directly from the students about their experiences, but also to watch the changes as they progress in maturity. As we discussed in the chapter on humility, we often worry about GT students thinking they're superior in some way, and it is tempting to remind them otherwise. But as we listen to them grow older, we see that time is a good teacher and helps them to put things in proper perspective, and maturity catches up to ability.

We can also see that each child speaks from his own experiences. Just as gifted children have different passions and interests, they also have different expectations, needs, and priorities.

The really cool part is that you don't have to guess and hope that you accidentally hit a home run with your eyes closed. All you have to do is ask!

Wait a minute! Okay, maybe that's not all you have to do. Some kids have a difficult time communicating in the traditional manner or don't feel comfortable expressing their needs vocally. They may need to write their feelings down on paper. They may need to communicate with someone they trust and who has already established a relationship with them.

But the point is that the answers for any given child are found within that child. Books on giftedness will help. Knowledge of general traits of gifted individuals will help you to know what to look for. Knowledge of techniques to help you meet their needs is critical. However, don't forget that the most important source for information on what a student needs is the student herself. You can't translate any of the other knowledge into solutions without knowing the individual.

Don't just take our word for it. You've got some pretty Intelligent Life in that classroom of yours. Ask the students!

Gifted Education Resources

Websites

Association for the Education of Gifted Underachieving Students
www.aegus.org

Belin-Blank Center for Gifted Education and Talent Development
www.education.uiowa.edu/belinblank

The Center for Gifted Education
http://cfge.wm.edu

Center for Gifted Education Policy (subsidiary of the American Psychological Association)
www.apa.org/ed/cgep.html

Center for Talented Youth
www.jhu.edu/gifted

Council for Exceptional Children – The Association for the Gifted
www.cectag.org

The Davidson Institute
www.ditd.org

Genius Denied
www.geniusdenied.com

Gifted Development Center
www.gifteddevelopment.com

Hoagies' Gifted Education Page
www.hoagiesgifted.org

Jacob K. Javits Gifted and Talented Students Education Program
www.ed.gov/programs/javits/index.html

A Nation Deceived: How Schools Hold Back America's Brightest Students
http://nationdeceived.org

The National Association for Gifted Children (includes links to all
state gifted association websites)
www.nagc.org

The National Research Center on the Gifted and Talented
www.gifted.uconn.edu/nrcgt.html

Neag Center for Gifted Education and Talent Development
www.gifted.uconn.edu

Renzulli Learning
www.renzullilearning.com

The Study of Mathematically Precocious Youth
www.vanderbilt.edu/Peabody/SMPY/default.htm

Supporting the Emotional Needs of the Gifted
www.sengifted.org

Teachers First
www.teachersfirst.com/gifted.shtml

The World Council for Gifted and Talented Children, Inc.
www.worldgifted.ca

Books for Teachers of Gifted Students

Active Questioning: Questioning Still Makes the Difference, by Nancy L. Johnson. This resource is full of activities that teach higher-order thinking skills through the formation of different kinds of questions. (1996, Pieces of Learning).

Assessment: Time-Saving Procedures for Busy Teachers, by Bertie Kingore. This book focuses on classroom applications and instructional tools. The objective is to make assessment efficient and integrated with instruction. (1999, Professional Associates).

Being Smart about Gifted Children: A Guidebook for Parents and Educators, by Dona Matthews and Joanne Foster. Contains advice and strategies to help educators identify and nurture the abilities of gifted children. Pre-assessment is emphasized as a strategy that enables teachers to provide educational experiences that a given child might need at a particular time. (2005, Great Potential Press).

Brain Stations: A Center Approach to Thinking Skills, by Greta Rasmussen. Perfect for the regular classroom grades K-5, this resource is full of ideas for centers that promote the development of higher-order thinking skills. (1989, Tin Man Press).

Challenge Math: For the Elementary and Middle School Student, by Edward Zaccaro. With chapters on statistics, probability, trigonometry, algebra, and much more, this great resource is full of challenging problems for grades 1-8 students who crave harder math. Each problem includes challenging extensions in Level 1, Level 2, and the Einstein Level. (2005, Hickory Grove Press).

College Planning for Gifted Students, by Sandra L. Berger. A valuable resource with a wide selection of information about college planning, specifically those issues of most relevance to gifted students as they make plans for education beyond high school. (2006, Prufrock Press).

Coping for Capable Kids: Strategies for Parents, Teachers, and Students, by LeoNora M. Cohen and Erica Frydenberg. A thorough look at many issues and problems common to gifted kids, plus strategies for how to deal with them. Includes chapters on perfectionism, boredom, underachievement, drug and alcohol use, anorexia and bulimia, depression and suicide, developing social skills, meta-cognition, emotional development, goal setting, coping with change, family functioning, dealing with feeling different, and many others. (2006, Prufrock Press).

Crossover Children: A Sourcebook for Helping Children Who Are Gifted and Learning Disabled, by Marlene Bireley. This sourcebook includes chapters on the crossover concept (gifted/learning disabled), educational planning and programming, behavioral and social interventions, academic interventions, and academic enrichment. (1995, Council for Exceptional Children).

Curriculum Compacting, by Sally Reis, Deborah Burns, and Joseph Renzulli. This book is widely recognized as the complete guide to modifying the regular curriculum for high-ability students. (1992, Creative Learning Press).

The Differentiated Classroom: Responding to the Needs of All Learners, by Carol Ann Tomlinson. This outstanding resource explains practical and tested strategies for curriculum differentiation in a variety of classroom grade levels and subjects. (1999, Association for Supervision and Curriculum Development).

Differentiation: Simplified, Realistic, and Effective, by Bertie Kingore. The focus of this book is to simplify the implementation of differentiation to increase its practice. Specific aids and examples are included that teachers have found particularly beneficial to simplify the planning and preparation process of differentiated instruction. (2004, Professional Associates).

Enrichment Clusters: A Practical Plan for Real-World, Student-Driven Learning, by Joseph Renzulli, Marcia Gentry, and Sally Reis. Student-driven enrichment clusters challenge the entire school family (students, teachers, staff, parents, and community volunteers) to investigate and engage in topics as professionals, applying advanced content and authentic methods to develop products and services for real-world audiences. Step-by-step guidelines show how to set up an Enrichment Cluster Program within the regular school week, train staff and community volunteers, create successful clusters, assess student products, evaluate the program, and more. (2003, Creative Learning Press).

The Faces of Gifted: A Resource for Educators and Parents, by Nancy L. Johnson. This book looks at differing perspectives of giftedness, characteristics of gifted children, right brain/left brain, creativity, discipline, gifted children at risk, parent advocacy, and a glossary for parents of terms often used in the field of gifted education. (1989, Creative Learning Consultants).

Genius Denied: How to Stop Wasting Our Brightest Young Minds, by Jan and Bob Davidson and Laura Vanderkam. An examination of the "quiet crisis" in America's schools—the academic neglect of the potential of our brightest students. (2005, Simon and Schuster).

Gifted and Talented Children in the Regular Classroom, by E. Paul Torrance and Dorothy A. Sisk. This book translates the most important research dealing with giftedness and creativity for use by all teachers and serves as the definitive resource for those committed to helping all students explore the vastness of their talents. Chapters focus on problems of educating gifted and talented children in the regular classroom, goals in teaching gifted and talented children, identifying and motivating gifted and talented children, curriculum for gifted and talented children, creative problem solving, cooperative learning, mentoring, and ways of individualizing instruction to use resources outside of the classroom. (1998, Pieces of Learning).

Gifted Children and Gifted Education, by Gary Davis. Written for regular classroom teachers, this is an easy-to-read, practical explanation of what is meant by the concept of giftedness and how parents and teachers can provide opportunities to develop abilities in young people. Describes gifted program options. Useful as a textbook or for teacher training. (2006, Great Potential Press).

The Gifted Kids' Survival Guide: For Ages 10 & Under, by Judy Galbraith. A wonderful handbook for young gifted children, this book offers tips on how to deal with teasing and perfectionism, how to make school more challenging and interesting, what it means to be gifted, and other topics of interest and importance to young, able learners. (1998, Free Spirit Publishing).

The Gifted Kids' Survival Guide: A Teen Handbook, by Judy Galbraith and Jim Delisle. This comprehensive handbook for teenaged gifted students provides information and tips about what it means to be gifted; identifying different forms of intelligence; being a teenager; taking charge of one's education; and developing peer, sibling, and parent relationships; as well as many other factors of importance and interest to gifted teens. (1996, Free Spirit Publishing).

Guiding the Gifted Child: A Practical Source for Parents and Teachers, by James T. Webb, Elizabeth A. Meckstroth, and Stephanie S. Tolan. A classic. Among the most widely read resources for parents and teachers of gifted children, this book offers information on motivation, discipline, stress management, communication of feelings, tradition breaking, depression, and parent, peer, and sibling relationships. (1982, Great Potential Press).

Helping Gifted Children Soar: A Practical Guide for Parents and Teachers, by Carol Strip and Gretchen Hirsch. A user-friendly guidebook about important gifted issues. Helpful for teacher and parent training. Describes "the basics" of gifted children and gifted education. (2000, Great Potential Press).

How the Gifted Brain Learns, by David A. Sousa. Helps turn research on the brain function of intellectually and creatively advanced students into practical classroom activities and strategies. Examines how the gifted brain is different and which strategies are effective for children with particular gifts. (2002, Corwin Press).

How to Differentiate Instruction in Mixed-Ability Classrooms, by Carol Ann Tomlinson. An in-depth look at how to match the curriculum to student interest, ability, and readiness. (2004, Prentice Hall).

In Search of the Dream: Designing Schools and Classrooms that Work for High Potential Students from Diverse Cultural Backgrounds, by Carol Ann Tomlinson, Donna Ford, Sally Reis, Christine Briggs, and Cindy Strickland. Contains a summary of research examining which styles of gifted programming and identification work best for students from diverse backgrounds, and also contains description and contact information for model programs from around the country that have been recognized for their successful means of meeting the needs of diverse gifted students. (2004, National Association for Gifted Children and the National Research Center on the Gifted and Talented). Available from NAGC at their website: www.nagc.org/acb/stores/1/In-Search-of-the-Dream-P111C31.aspx.

The Kingore Observation Inventory, by Bertie Kingore. A complete handbook that explains the KOI and also includes activities teachers can use with their classes that will highlight some or all of the traits under observation. (2001, Professional Associates).

Literature Links: Activities for Gifted Readers, by Teresa Masiello. Differentiation in reading. A good description of how to work with regular and advanced readers, grades 2-6, using groups and activities. Ten well-loved titles, like *Frederick* and *Freaky Friday,* serve as examples for classroom use, with questions and activities for students to complete individually or in small groups. Strategies include graphic organizers, literature binders, portfolios, and more. Activities adapt to other books. (2006, Great Potential Press).

Looking for Data in All the Right Places: A Guidebook for Conducting Original Research with Young Investigators, by Alane J. Starko and Gina D. Schack. This resource is a complete guide to teaching students how to conduct descriptive, historical, experimental, correlational, and developmental research, plus how to gather data by observation, survey, interview, and document analysis. (1991, Creative Learning Press).

Losing Our Minds: Gifted Children Left Behind, by Deborah L. Ruf. An examination of different types and levels of giftedness, plus strategies for distinguishing between them and meeting their needs. Contains helpful information on tests, pros and cons of different tests used for gifted identification, test scoring and interpretation, and problems with test ceilings. Anecdotal data and test data from more than 50 highly and profoundly gifted children include the children's early developmental milestones and IQ test scores. (2005, Great Potential Press).

Managing the Social and Emotional Needs of the Gifted: A Teacher's Survival Guide, by Connie C. Schmitz and Judy Galbraith. This book is about understanding, living with, and encouraging social and emotional growth among gifted, talented, and creative youth. It provides parents, teachers, and counselors with current research, support, and more than 30 practical strategies for helping students to gain insights, find solutions, and understand that they are not alone. Offers tips on how to help students resolve conflicts, take responsibility for their learning, develop strategies for managing stress, and understand and accept themselves and others. (1985, Free Spirit Publishing).

Misdiagnosis and Dual Diagnosis of Gifted Children and Adults: ADHD, Bipolar, OCD, Asperger's, Depression, and Other Disorders, by James T. Webb, Edward R. Amend, Nadia E. Webb, Jean Goerss, Paul Beljan, and F. Richard Olenchak. The traits and characteristics of giftedness share some similarities with various disorders, yet the psychologists or MDs who diagnose these disorders receive no training in their educations about traits of giftedness and the similarities to these disorders, nor how to distinguish between the two. As a result, gifted children and adults around the country have been misdiagnosed as having one of these (or other) disorders. This important text is the first to differentiate how giftedness and these disorders are actually separate and distinct. While it is possible for an individual to be gifted and also have one of these disorders (some do), it's important for parents, teachers, and psychologists to know the differences so that a mistaken diagnosis is not made, and so that an accurate diagnoses *is* made. (2005, Great Potential Press).

Motivating the Gifted Child, by Carol Strip and Gretchen Hirsch. This book discusses causes for loss of motivation, including physical, emotional, social, physical, and school reasons. Suggestions for enhancing motivation include control, challenge, compassion, and commitment. Advice for motivating every student. (2007, Great Potential Press).

A Nation Deceived: How Schools Hold Back America's Brightest Students, by Nicholas Colangelo, Susan G. Assouline, and Miraca U. M. Gross. A thorough compilation of 50+ years of comprehensive research on student acceleration. It contains articles, research statistics, and an important discussion of the nuts and bolts of acceleration issues. In particular, the materi̇ä documents the overwhelming evidence that appropriate acceleration has positive benefits for gifted students. (2004, Templeton National Report on Education).

On the Social and Emotional Lives of Gifted Children, by Tracy L. Cross. A researcher and administrator at a school for gifted students, Tracy Cross has written many articles for *Gifted Child Today* magazine. This book is a compilation of those articles on topics ranging from "Examining Beliefs about the Gifted" to "Guiding and Supporting the Development of Gifted Children" to "The Lived Experiences of Gifted Students in School" and many others. (2005, Prufrock Press).

The Parallel Curriculum: A Model for Planning Curriculum for Gifted Students and Whole Classrooms, by Carol Ann Tomlinson, Sandra N. Kaplan, Joseph Renzulli, Deborah E. Burns, Jann H. Leppien, and Jeanne H. Purcell. The four parallel approaches to curriculum development illustrate ascending intellectual demand as a means of extending the intensity of challenge for students as they work toward expertise in learning. This book provides practical guidelines for developing a rich curriculum for all learners. (2001, Corwin Press).

A Parent's Guide to Gifted Children, by James Webb, Janet Gore, Edward Amend, and Arlene DeVries. This book outlines some of the common characteristics and behaviors of gifted children. The authors give advice for dealing with asynchrony, intensity, sensitivity, idealism, perfectionism, motivation or lack of motivation, friendship, discipline, and more. (2007, Great Potential Press).

Perfectionism: What's Bad about Being Too Good? by Miriam Adderholdt-Elliott. This book helps to distinguish between healthy and unhealthy forms of perfectionism, plus offers information on why people become perfectionists, what perfectionism does to the mind and body, and what perfectionism does to relationships. Also included are tips on how to ease up on oneself, ways to realistically gain control over one's life, learning to savor success, and when and how to get help with coping. (1999, Free Spirit Publishing).

Plexers: Arithmetic, by David Hammond, Tom Lester, and Joe Scales. Perfect for math classrooms of grades 6-12, this resource offers 270+ *highly* challenging word puzzles that all relate to mathematics. (2000, Dale Seymour Publications).

Plexers: Science, by David Hammond, Tom Lester, and Joe Scales. Perfect for science classrooms of grades 6-12, this resource offers 284 *highly* challenging word puzzles that all relate to science, including the areas of biology, chemistry, geology, meteorology, and physics. (1999, Dale Seymour Publications).

Plexers: Social Studies, by David Hammond, Tom Lester, and Joe Scales. Perfect for history and social studies classrooms of grades 6-12, this resource offers 273 *highly* challenging word puzzles that all relate to social studies, including the areas of anthropology, government, history, politics, and sociology. (1999, Dale Seymour Publications).

Primary Education Thinking Skills: A Curriculum for Higher Level Thinking, by Jody Nichols. Created for K-2 classrooms, this series of books includes hundreds of activities that promote the development of convergent, divergent, visual, and evaluative thinking skills. (1997, Pieces of Learning).

Questioning Makes the Difference, by Nancy L. Johnson. This resource is full of activities that teach higher-order thinking skills through the formation of different kinds of questions. (1990, Pieces of Learning).

Raisin' Brains: Surviving My Smart Family, by Karen L. J. Isaacson. A witty and humorous look at one mother's house full of gifted children. Laugh out loud with her and her family. (2002, Great Potential Press).

Re-Forming Gifted Education: How Parents and Teachers Can Match the Program to the Child, by Karen B. Rogers. From her analysis of research that spans a full century, the author describes various types of gifted children, as well as options for school enrichment and acceleration and the effectiveness of each option. Also shown are practical ways to design ongoing programs that best meet the needs of bright children. (2002, Great Potential Press).

Removing the Mask: Giftedness in Poverty, by Ruby Payne and Paul Slocumb. One volume from Ruby's renowned collection of works on students from poverty, this book focuses on gifted students who live in poverty and how best to identify them. The book also provides a wealth of examples of the unique needs and issues of gifted students who come from impoverished backgrounds. (2000, RFT Publications).

Scamper and *Scamper On: Creative Games and Activities for Imagination Development*, by Bob Eberle. Adaptable to any grade level, these activities promote the development of creativity and imagination. (1997, Prufrock Press).

The Schoolwide Enrichment Model: A How-To Guide for Educational Excellence (2nd ed.), by Joseph Renzulli and Sally Reis. The Schoolwide Enrichment model is an excellent way for schools to both provide services to gifted students and nurture the talents and interests of all students. (1997, Creative Learning Press).

Smart Boys: Talent, Manhood, and the Search for Meaning, by Barbara A. Kerr and Sanford J. Cohn. Incorporates the most recent research findings about gifted boys of all ages, the obstacles of the "Boy Code," and how parents, teachers, and counselors can help guide gifted boys toward actualizing their talents. (2001, Great Potential Press).

Smart Girls: A New Psychology of Girls, Women, and Giftedness, by Barbara A. Kerr. Incorporates the most recent research findings about gifted girls of all ages, eminent women, and how parents, teachers, and counselors can help guide gifted girls toward actualizing their talents.Practical advice for parents and teachers on how to help gifted girls grow and succeed. (2000, Great Potential Press).

The Social and Emotional Development of Gifted Children: What Do We Know? edited by Maureen Neihart, Sally Reis, Nancy Robinson, and Sidney Moon. A service publication of the National Association for Gifted Children, this book summarizes and highlights all of the best and most current research regarding the social and emotional development of gifted children. More than 20 specific topics are covered. (2001, Prufrock Press).

Some of My Best Friends Are Books: Guiding Gifted Readers from Pre-School to High School, by Judith Wynn Halsted. This guide for parents, teachers, librarians, and counselors offers updated background information on the emotional and intellectual needs of gifted children, describes typical reading patterns of high-ability readers and their need for reading guidance, and includes an annotated bibliography of more than 300 books carefully selected to be useful in promoting the intellectual and emotional development of high-ability children. (2002, Great Potential Press).

T is for Think: Thinking Fun with the Alphabet, by Greta and Ted Rasmussen. A creative resource for K-2 teachers, each page of this book contains thoughtful challenges for use with a different letter of the alphabet. (1995, Tin Man Press).

Teaching Gifted Kids in the Regular Classroom, by Susan Winebrenner. This book offers strategies and techniques every teacher can use to meet the academic needs of gifted and talented students in the regular classroom. It includes information on curriculum compacting and contracting for various subject areas, cluster grouping, characteristic behaviors of gifted and talented students, ways to create more challenging activities for gifted students, and more. A CD-ROM of customizable forms in the book is also available. (2000, Free Spirit Publishing).

Teaching Young Gifted Children in the Regular Classroom: Identifying, Nurturing, and Challenging Ages 4-9, by Joan Franklin Smutny, Sally Yahnke Walker, and Elizabeth A. Meckstroth. This excellent resource provides information on identifying the young gifted child; creating a challenging learning environment; compacting the curriculum; promoting creativity, discovery, and critical thinking; and understanding and meeting a young gifted child's social and emotional needs, plus more. (1997, Free Spirit Publishing).

Teen Success: Jump Start Ideas to Move Your Mind, by Beatrice Elyè. Useful suggestions for pre-teens and teens to jumpstart their minds, achieve goals, and appreciate their lives. Can be used to lead seminars on various topics or for teens to read themselves. Topics include speed reading, time management, organization, self-esteem, confidence, courage, ambition, solitude, and more. (2000, Great Potential Press).

Thinking Is the Key: Questioning Makes the Difference, by Nancy L. Johnson. This practical resource for teaching critical thinking includes hundreds of divergent questions and activities to supplement the basic curriculum. (1992, Pieces of Learning).

To Be Gifted and Learning Disabled, by Susan M. Baum, Steven V. Owen, and John Dixon. The gifted and learning disabled child exhibits remarkable talents in some areas and disabling weaknesses in others. This book covers the research behind this phenomenon and strategies to assist parents, teachers, and students who struggle with this challenge. (2004, Creative Learning Press).

Understanding Creativity, by Jane Piirto. A thorough examination of the qualities and characteristics most common to highly creative individuals, as well as an analysis of just what it is that drives them to create. Creativity in all areas is covered, including the arts, sciences, and mathematics. (2004, Great Potential Press).

Upside-Down Brilliance: The Visual-Spatial Learner, by Linda Kreger Silverman. A description of students whose strengths lie in the visual-spatial realm. (2002, De Leon Publishing).

When Gifted Kids Don't Have All the Answers: How to Meet Their Social and Emotional Needs, by James Delisle and Judy Galbraith. A comprehensive compilation for any adult who lives or works with gifted students, this book offers practical suggestions for encouraging social and emotional growth among gifted kids. Based on classroom experience, survey data, current research, and contributions from students, it explains what giftedness means and how gifted kids are identified. It also focuses on ways to create a supportive environment for all gifted students, ways to advocate for gifted education, and covers many social/emotional issues common to gifted youth, including perfectionism, boredom, and underachievement. (2002, Free Spirit Publishing).

Why Bright Kids Get Poor Grades: And What You Can Do about It—A Six-Step Program for Parents and Teachers, by Silvia Rimm. Underachieving gifted students are a complex and confusing phenomenon to most adults. How is it that such capable children can sometimes not do well in school? This book analyzes the factors contributing to underachievement and outlines a plan for how parents and teachers can help get these students back on track. (1996, Three Rivers Press).

You Know Your Child Is Gifted When...: A Beginner's Guide to Life on the Bright Side, by Judy Galbraith. This book blends humorous cartoons with solid information on giftedness—its characteristics, challenges, and joys—plus reassuring and insightful first-person stories from parents who have been there. (2000, Free Spirit Publishing).

Magazines and Journals

Creative Kids available from Prufrock Press
www.prufrock.com/client/client_pages/prufrock_jm_createkids.cfm

Gifted Child Today available from Prufrock Press.
www.prufrock.com/client/client_pages/prufrock_jm_giftchild.cfm

Gifted Education Communicator available from the California Association for the Gifted
www.cagifted.org/Pages/Publications/communicator.html

Imagine... available from the Center for Talented Youth
http://cty.jhu.edu/imagine

Teaching for High Potential available from the National Association for Gifted Children.
www.nagc.org/index.aspx?id=563

Twice-Exceptional Newsletter available from Glen Ellyn Media
www.2enewsletter.com

Understanding Our Gifted available from Open Space Communications
www.openspacecomm.com/OSCUOG.htm

Catalogs/Companies with Gifted Education Materials

ALPS Publishing
P.O. Box 336052
Greeley, CO 80633
Phone: (800) 345-2577
Fax: (970) 353-0260
Email: ALPSpublishing@comcast.net
www.alpspublishing.com

Bright Ideas for the Gifted and Talented
A. W. Peller & Associates, Inc.
116 Washington Avenue
P.O. Box 106
Hawthorne, NJ 07507-0106
Phone: (800) 451-7450
Fax: (973) 423-5569
Email: awpeller@optonline.net
www.awpeller.com

Corwin Press
2455 Teller Road
Thousand Oaks, CA 91320-2218
(800) 818-7243
www.CorwinPress.com

Creative Learning Press, Inc.
P.O. Box 320
Mansfield Center, CT 06250
Phone: (888) 518-8004
Fax: (860) 429-7783
Email: clp@creativelearningpress.com
www.creativelearningpress.com

The Critical Thinking Co.
P.O. Box 1610
Seaside, CA 93955-1610
Phone: (800) 458-4849
Fax: (831) 393-3277
www.criticalthinking.com

Engine-Uity, Ltd.
P.O. Box 9610
Phoenix, AZ 85068
Phone: (800) 877-8718
Fax: (602) 997-0974
Email: support@engine-uity.com
www.engine-uity.com

Free Spirit Publishing
217 Fifth Avenue North, Suite 200
Minneapolis, MN 55401-1299
Phone: (800) 735-7323
Fax: (612) 337-5050
www.freespirit.com

Great Potential Press
P.O. Box 5057
Scottsdale AZ 85261
Phone: (877) 954-4200
Fax: (602) 954-0185
Email: info@giftedbooks.com
www.giftedbooks.com

Interact
W5527 State Road 106
P.O. Box 900
Fort Atkinson, WI 53538-0900
(800) 359-0961
www.teachinteract.com

Math Channel
701 Cottage Grove Road, Suite E-20
Bloomfield, CT 06002
Phone: (860) 808-0570
Fax: (860) 808-1410
www.mathchannel.com

MindWare
2100 County Road C W
Roseville, MN 55113
Phone: (800) 999-0398
Fax: (888)299-9273
Email: info@MindWareOnline.com
www.MINDWAREonline.com

Muggins! Math
4860 Burnt Mountain Road
Ellijay, GA 30540
Phone: (800) 962-8849
Fax: (706) 635-7611
Email: muggings@mugginsmath.com
www.mugginsmath.com

Pieces of Learning
Division of Creative Learning Consultants, Inc.
1990 Market Road
Marion, IL 62959
Phone: (800) 729-5137
Fax: (800) 844-0455
Email: piecesoflearning@verizon.net
www.piecesoflearning.com

Prufrock Press, Inc.
P.O. Box 8813
Waco, TX 76714-8813
Phone: (800) 998-2208
Fax: (800) 240-0333
www.prufrock.com

Zanca
351 Concord Road
Northfield, NH 03276
Phone: (800) 397-4156
Fax: (603) 286-2092
Email: zanca@zancas.com
www.zancas.com

Zephyr Press
814 N. Franklin Street
Chicago, IL 60610
Phone: (800) 232-2187
Fax: (312) 337-5985
Email: zephyrpress@zephyrpress.com
www.zephyrpress.com

Gifted Education Conferences

Association for the Education of Gifted Underachieving Students (AEGUS) Conference
www.aegus.org

Autonomous Learner Model (ALM) Conference
www.alpspublishing.com

Confratute
www.gifted.uconn.edu/confratute

Edufest
www.edufest.org

National Association for Gifted Children (NAGC) Conference
www.nagc.org

Supporting Emotional Needs of the Gifted (SENG) Conference
www.sengifted.org/conference_about.shtml

World Council for Gifted and Talented Children Conference
www.worldgifted.ca

Please contact your state gifted association for information about your own state's gifted education conference!

Competitions for Kids
(though National Programs/Foundations)

Destination Imagination
P.O. Box 547
Glassboro, NJ 08028
Phone: (856) 881-1603
Fax: (856) 881-3596
Email: askdi@dihq.org
www.destinationimagination.org

The Dupont Challenge
c/o General Learning Communications
900 Skokie Blvd., Suite 200
Northbrook, IL 60062-4028
www.glcomm.com/dupont

Future Problem Solving Program
2015 Grant Place
Melbourne, FL 32901
Phone: (800) 256-1499
Fax: (321) 768-0097
Email: mail@fpsp.org
www.fpsp.org

Intel Science Talent Search
Science Service
1719 N Street N.W.
Washington, DC 20036
(202) 785-2255
www.sciserv.org/sts/index.asp

Invent America!
United States Patent Model Foundation
P.O. Box 26065
Alexandria, VA 22313
Phone: (703) 942-7121
Fax: (703) 461-0068
Email: inquiries@inventamerica.org
www.inventamerica.org

MATHCOUNTS
MathCounts Foundation
1420 King Street
Alexandria, VA 22314
Phone: (703) 684-2828
Fax: (703) 836-4875
Email: info@mathcounts.org
www.mathcounts.org

National Geography Bee
National Geographic Society
1145 17th Street N.W.
Washington, D.C. 20036-4688
www.nationalgeographic.com/geographybee/basics.html

National History Day
0119 Cecil Hall
University of Maryland
College Park, MD 20742
(301) 314-9739
www.nationalhistoryday.org

Odyssey of the Mind
c/o Creative Competitions, Inc.
1325 Route 130 South, Suite F
Gloucester City, NJ 08030
Phone: (856) 456-7776
Fax: (856) 456-7008
www.odysseyofthemind.com

Siemens Westinghouse Competitions
in Math, Science, and Technology
Siemens Foundation
170 Wood Avenue South
Iselin, NJ 08830
Phone: (877) 822-5233
Fax: (732) 603-5890
Email: foundation.us@siemens.com
www.siemens-foundation.org

ThinkQuest
c/o Oracle Education Foundation
500 Oracle Parkway
Mailstop 5OP-8
Redwood Shores, CA 94065
www.thinkquest.org

Toshiba/NSTA ExploraVision Awards
1840 Wilson Blvd.
Arlington, VA 22201-3000
(800) EXPLOR9
Email: exploravision@nsta.org
www.exploravision.org

Voice of Democracy
VFW National Headquarters
406 West 34th Street
Kansas City, MO 64111
Phone: (816) 968-1117
Fax: (816) 968-1149
www.vfw.org/index.cfm?fa=cmty.leveld&did=150

Visit http://cty.jhu.edu/imagine/linkB.htm for lists of many more contests!

# Endnotes

1   A delightful novel by Frank Gilbreth about a family with 12 children.

2   Ovaltine® is a powdered, chocolate-flavored drink that was popular in the U.S. in the 1950s and 60s. It originated in Switzerland and can be found in countries worldwide now.

3   Leon Lederman (1922-) won the 1988 Nobel Prize in physics. In addition to being a professor and particle physicist, he also founded the Illinois Mathematics and Science Academy, Illinois's first statewide residential public school for gifted children.

4   Knowledge Master Open is an online competition where teams of students answer curriculum-based questions. The KMO website is www.greatauk.com.

5   Western Blotting is basically a method for detecting specific proteins in tissue samples. The process electronically moves proteins through a fine, porous gel. The proteins move at a specific rate through the gel, with the smallest going the farthest and so on. Based on this test, the proteins can be distinguished by their size, weight, and antibodies. Western Blotting is used to detect diseases such as HIV, BSE (commonly known as "mad cow disease"), and Lyme disease.

6   Historically, ninjas were Japanese agents of espionage and assassination, but they are now shown in Western fiction as expert martial artists. They are popular in the form of children's toys, originally as Ninja Turtles®, a cartoon from the 1980s.

7   Nikola Tesla (1856-1943) was an inventor and electrical and mechanical engineer. He was the first to develop alternating current and secured a number of patents for devices which used this new technology.

8   Harriet Tubman (c.1820-1913) was a former slave who became well-known for directing hundreds of other slaves from the South to safety in the North via a network of safe houses and hiding places called the Underground Railroad.

9   Tao is the Chinese character for "road" or "path."

10   Mihaly Csikszentmihalyi (1934-) is a psychology professor who has written several books about creativity and happiness. This quote comes from his 2006 book, *Creativity: Flow and the Psychology of Discovery and Invention* (New York: HarperCollins).

11   J.K. Rowling (1965-) is the author of the popular Harry Potter series of books for children, starting with *Harry Potter and the Sorcerer's Stone™*, released in 1997.

12   The limiting reactant here is graham crackers because two are needed for each s'more. A s'more consists of two graham crackers, one marshmallow (unless you're not on a diet!), and one chocolate square. In the professor's problem, the four graham crackers will be used up before all of the eight marshmallows and six chocolate squares are used up. This formula would have six leftover marshmallows and four leftover chocolate squares.

13   Jules Verne (1828-1905), French novelist, is considered one of the founders of the science fiction genre.

14   General George Patton (1885-1945) was an American general in WWII. He commanded the 3rd Army dash across France and into Germany following the D-Day Invasion.

15   Thomas Alva Edison (1847-1931) is best known for his invention of the lightbulb. His other important inventions include the telegraph, phonograph, and improvements to an electric distribution system. At the time of his death, he had patented more than 1,000 inventions.

16 Braille is a system of raised dots which allows blind people to read words and numbers in text. It was developed by Louis Braille in 1829. There are also Braille codes for music and mathematics.

17 Emily Dickinson (1830-1886) was an American poet who wrote nearly 1,800 short lyrics, with only seven published in her lifetime. Her collected works were not published until 1955. Her poems speak of emotion and sensitivity to simple things.

18 CSI stands for "Crime Scene Investigation" and is a popular television show in America which features a group of forensic scientists who use their scientific skills and knowledge to solve crimes.

19 Copyright© 1997, Apple Computer Company.

About the Authors

Karen Isaacson is the mother of five weird and wonderful gifted children. She grew up surrounded by siblings and relatives who were equally as quirky and has learned through much experience that "different is good." Karen is the author of the award-winning book *Raisin' Brains: Surviving My Smart Family*. She has presented her humorous take on parenting gifted children at state and national conferences. She currently lives in southwestern Montana, where she enjoys gardening, antiques, and plenty of laughter. Karen is married to a left-brained perfectionist-in-denial who is supportive of every creative activity she chooses to pursue. Learn more about Karen at www.kisaacson.com

Tamara Fisher is the K-12 Gifted Education Specialist for a school district located on an Indian Reservation in northwestern Montana. Tamara made her first mark on the world of Gifted Education as an undergraduate when she co-created a volunteer mentor program matching gifted college students with gifted youth, a program that still exists today. She serves as the Northwest Regional Representative on the Executive Board of Montana AGATE (Association of Gifted and Talented Education). Tamara earned her B.S. in Elementary Education from Montana State University-Bozeman and her M.A. in Gifted Education from the University of Connecticut. She has presented at many local, state, and national Gifted Education conferences. Her hobbies include building houses, drawing, hiking, four-wheeling, and spending time with family and friends. Learn more about Tamara at www.thethinkteacher.com.